# Body Factory

In the series *Sporting*, edited by Amy Bass

ALSO IN THIS SERIES:

Samir Chopra, *The Evolution of a Cricket Fan: My Shapeshifting Journey*
Rebecca Joyce Kissane and Sarah Winslow, *Whose Game? Gender and Power in Fantasy Sports*
Charles K. Ross, *Mavericks, Money, and Men: The AFL, Black Players, and the Evolution of Modern Football*
Yago Colás, *Ball Don't Lie! Myth, Genealogy, and Invention in the Cultures of Basketball*
Thomas P. Oates and Zack Furness, eds., *The NFL: Critical and Cultural Perspectives*
David L. Andrews and Michael L. Silk, eds., *Sporting and Neoliberalism: Politics, Consumption, and Culture*
David Wangerin, *Distant Corners: American Soccer's History of Missed Opportunities and Lost Causes*
Zack Furness, *One Less Car: Bicycling and the Politics of Automobility*
Michael Ezra, *Muhammad Ali: The Making of an Icon*
Thomas Hauser, *The Boxing Scene*
David Wangerin, *Soccer in a Football World: The Story of America's Forgotten Game*
Grant Farred, *Long Distance Love: A Passion for Football*
Tommie Smith, *Silent Gesture: The Autobiography of Tommie Smith*

KAITLIN PERICAK

# Body Factory

*Exploiting University Athletes' Healthcare for Profit in the Training Room*

TEMPLE UNIVERSITY PRESS
*Philadelphia* • *Rome* • *Tokyo*

TEMPLE UNIVERSITY PRESS
Philadelphia, Pennsylvania 19122
tupress.temple.edu

Copyright © 2025 by Temple University—Of The Commonwealth System
of Higher Education
All rights reserved
Published 2025

Library of Congress Cataloging-in-Publication Data

Names: Pericak, Kaitlin, 1992– author.
Title: Body factory : exploiting university athletes' healthcare for profit in the training room / Kaitlin Pericak.
Other titles: Sporting (Philadelphia, Pa.)
Description: Philadelphia : Temple University Press, 2025. | Series: Sporting | Includes bibliographical references and index. | Summary: "This book provides an ethnography of an athletic training center in the athletics department of an NCAA Division I University in the United States. The author argues that the organizational orientation towards profit leads staff to use social structures to promote control and surveillance over individual care or empowerment"— Provided by publisher.
Identifiers: LCCN 2024016393 (print) | LCCN 2024016394 (ebook) | ISBN 9781439924938 (cloth) | ISBN 9781439924945 (paperback) | ISBN 9781439924952 (pdf)
Subjects: LCSH: College athletes—Health and hygiene—United States—Case studies. | Sports injuries—Treatment—United States—Case studies. | Sports medicine—United States—Case studies. | College sports—Economic aspects—United States—Case studies. | Physical education and training—United States—Administration—Case studies.
Classification: LCC GV351 .P47 2025 (print) | LCC GV351 (ebook) | DDC 617.1/0270973—dc23/eng/20240903
LC record available at https://lccn.loc.gov/2024016393
LC ebook record available at https://lccn.loc.gov/2024016394

9 8 7 6 5 4 3 2 1

*To my parents, Arlene and Bill.*

# Contents

Acknowledgments ix
List of Abbreviations xi

Introduction 1
1. College Athlete Healthcare 20
2. The Organization of NLU's Athletic Training Center 29
3. In-House Care 41
4. Sense-Making in the ATC 50
5. The Gendered Nature of Healthcare in Big-Time College Sport 62
6. The Racialized Nature of Healthcare in Big-Time College Sport 72
7. Intersectional Experiences in College Athlete Healthcare 79
8. Recognition of Injury 87
9. Uncertainty of Injury 97
10. Mobilizing Resources for Injury 103
    Conclusion 113

Appendixes 123
References 129
Index 141

## Acknowledgments

This book would not be possible without my entire support system. First, I want to thank my graduate school adviser and mentor, Dr. Kathryn Nowotny. This project stemmed from a series of conversations we had over the years and was greatly influenced by your critical and medical sociological perspective.

Thank you to Dr. John Murphy for your theoretical expertise that guided much of the work in this book.

Thank you to my mentor Dr. Rick Eckstein for all your help in seeing this project through all the way to the end.

To my students, thank you for critically engaging with me in class and being thought-provoking during this process.

Thank you to all the athletes I had the pleasure of coaching over the years, your insights helped me be a better coach, and, in turn, a better sport scholar.

And last, but certainly not least, thank you to my family and friends for your constant support in all that I do.

# List of Abbreviations

| | |
|---|---|
| ACL | Anterior Cruciate Ligament |
| ACSM | American College of Sports Medicine |
| ATC | Athletic Training Center |
| CRT | Critical Race Theory |
| CT | Computerized Tomography |
| DI | Division I |
| DPT | Doctor of Physical Therapy |
| ESPN | Entertainment and Sports Programming Network |
| HEI | Higher Education Institution |
| MRI | Magnetic Resonance Imaging |
| NARP | Non-athletic Regular Person |
| NATA | National Athletic Training Association |
| NCAA | National Collegiate Athletic Association |
| NLU | Neoliberal University |
| PCL | Posterior Cruciate Ligament |
| PWI | Predominantly White Institution |
| STIM | Electrical Stimulation Therapy |

Body Factory

# Introduction

In theory, the people in a college athletic training room have a simple goal: to care for and heal the athletes who depend on that space. And that unifying orientation is on the minds of staff. In an interview with Noah, an athletic trainer at Neoliberal University (NLU), a university with big-time sports, he discusses the role of sports medicine staff members in college athlete healthcare:

> You have to be able to listen; you have to be able to understand what's going on. The bottom line is that we all have to have the same goal, which is the care of the athlete. Because then everything works out well.

The "end goal" of college athlete healthcare as he describes it, is to make sure athletes are receiving the care they need. This is a common theme in discussions with sports medicine staff members at this university. The emphasis is put first and foremost on caring for the athlete. Similarly, in describing her position, Maria, an athletic trainer at the same university, states:

So, my job really comes down to helping facilitate medical [care] for the well-being of the student-athlete. So, athlete well-being across the board. I kind of just make sure all the little bits are running smoothly that still relate to the student-athlete welfare, health, and safety.

The approach that Noah and Maria are referring to is what the National Collegiate Athletic Association (NCAA) calls "athlete-centered care" (Courson et al. 2014; NCAA 2021a), which is similar to "patient-centered care," a term coined by Enid Balint (1969) that refers to the practice where medical attention focuses on the patient's needs and concerns, as opposed to those of the doctors. Similarly, in athlete-centered care, the focus is on the athlete's needs as unique human beings. The NCAA (2024a) declares in its mission statement that it was founded in 1906 "to keep college athletes safe. The Association is still working hard to protect them physically and mentally." The place where athletes are to get these needs met and receive care is in the Athletic Training Center (ATC).

While the sincere goal of sports medicine staff members is to center athletes and provide the best healthcare possible, some organizational constraints affect this. Those constraints are based on not only resources, regulations, or anything material but also on the effects of the organization's actual social functions on the day-to-day interpersonal culture. One of these organizational constraints is the pressure sports medicine staff members feel both to get athletes back on the field, mainly the most valuable athletes—the athletes from the profit-generating sports—and to keep them healthy enough to perform. Although unexpressed, generating profit for the university is an important goal in this organization, the ATC, and, to successfully protect profit, power over the individual athlete must be maintained, lest the athlete pursues goals outside those of the organization, a challenge to the stated ethos of centering the athlete.

So, even though the NCAA states that it is centering athletes in its care, when injured athletes talk to us about their experiences in the ATC, some do not feel "centered." For example, Jack, a Black men's football athlete, felt pressured to play after experiencing a career-ending spinal cord injury. He discusses how he had "unbearable pain" and was having a hard time sleeping. Once he told his athletic trainer, he was taken to the medical director's home. Jack recounts:

> Before I went to the actual neck specialist, we went to [the medical director's] house, actually. Because as soon as I told [the athletic trainer], they immediately took me there. They wanted to be sure before I went to the neck specialist. They were like, are you sure? Are you sure you want to do this? Yeah, I'm okay with walking away from football and not risking my life.

While Jack received great care when he was able-bodied enough to be an asset to the men's football program, once he could no longer play, his sense was that interest in his care greatly diminished. He explains:

> I guess they're, like, disappointed because they have an image, a look. I guess they had a first-round talent, and now he's not like . . . the man.

If the ATC and NCAA college athlete healthcare *centers* the athlete as stated, then there should never be pressure put on athletes to continue to play when injured. Instead, centering the athlete would result in doing what is best for the athlete. However, athlete experiences show a disconnect between what the NCAA states as its goal of athlete healthcare and what is actually happening. In other words, describing the care as "athlete-centered" obscures the actual interactions that are occurring. In this system, profit-generating sport athletes become commodities. Despite the best of intentions of sports medicine staff members, instead of the athlete being centered, what is centered in this system is generating profit.

This system, the U.S. collegiate sport system, is a total institution—a term originating from the sociologist Erving Goffman (1961)—where athletes work and live allowing them to be surveilled and controlled. A total institution encases its occupants in the logics and rules of its governing system, cutting them off from the norms of the outside world. The sociologist Sarah Hatteberg (2018), sport scholars Richard Southall and Jonathon Weiler (2014), anthropologist Tracie Canada and colleagues (2022), and sport and health scholar Caitlin Vitosky Clarke and I (2023) have all applied Goffman's concept of a total institution to the U.S. collegiate sport system. Each of us, in our work, highlights the negative consequences of athletes being immersed in a total institution. Canada and colleagues (2022: 58) state, "Total institutions exist at multiple bureaucratic levels when considering college athletes: the NCAA, the universities, and the teams." An additional bureaucratic level is where athletes receive healthcare: the ATC. In this total institution of college sport we can find an example of what the sociologist Max Weber ([1904] 1958: 68–69) refers to as rationalization—structures are characterized by the most direct and efficient "means to its ends." In this regard, rationalization results in objectifying and commodifying the most valuable bodies to use in a manner to achieve the "ends" of the university, which is to generate profit.

## Follow the Money: Neoliberalism

Looking at the institutions involved, and the society at large that influences the institutions, the mechanisms that drive decisions in the ATC are based on the neoliberal paradigm. Neoliberalism emerged in the 1970s during a period of "stagflation" (Harvey 2005), but it was not until the 1980s that the term gained common use in Chile after students of Milton Friedman's at the University of Chicago staged a revolution (Valdés 1995).

This book draws on geographer David Harvey (2005: 19) who defines neoliberalism as a "political project to re-establish the conditions for capital accumulation and restore the power of economic elites." In the American university system, where colleges function as businesses, the university itself both accumulates money and power and is used in strategies for and by various stakeholders to maintain or gain capital and power. Neoliberalism is a political approach to society that is determined by a set of ideas that favor capitalism. These ideas or mantras include the use of a "free market" system, privatization, deregulation, and profit motivation. According to the anthropologist Sam Dubal (2010), neoliberalism has developed into a mode of governance that shifts social responsibility from the state to the individual, corporate, and NGO actors.

Neoliberalism, in theory, is argued to provide all people with the opportunity to be economically successful. However, neoliberalism fails to account for structural issues embedded in modern institutions, such as racism and sexism. Therefore, unregulated capitalism (neoliberalism) results in the exacerbation of social inequalities. So, while the neoliberal model supposedly allows all to have equal access to economic prosperity in the free market of capitalism, hidden structural constraints limit individual access to the value they may generate, which can be seen in the ATC as athletes struggle to access resources that ultimately accrue to the university as a direct result of their athletic labor. The sociologist Nathan Kalman-Lamb (2018: 72) argues that "in athletic labor, the athlete functions as both labor-power and the means of production, for the commodity is the athlete's performance, produced through the use of the body."

The organization of the ATC reflects the role of the larger university whose goals it advances, and those university goals navigate a still higher network of social structures that orient its actions. The social structures in place are embedded in and sustained by the dominant ideologies of masculinity and whiteness that affect the care being provided. To fully understand the injury experience in college sport, an observer must be conscious of the dominant ideologies and processes that have created the current system. Moreover, modern-day inequities cannot be fully understood without also considering the history that has created these conditions. Therefore, this Introduction gives a broad overview of the book and situates college athlete healthcare within NLU and the NCAA, part of the sports-industrial complex—a modern manifestation of capitalism and racial capitalism, made possible because of settler colonialism, anti-Black racism, and the neoliberal model.[1] Examining college athlete healthcare in the context of settler colonialism, capitalism and racial capitalism, anti-Black racism, and neoliberalism provides a clearer picture of college athlete healthcare since these ideas are embedded in sport, medical, and academic institutions (see Figure 0.1).

---

1. These processes are extremely complex, and the forthcoming sections are not in any way exhaustive. Rather, they provide limited information to set the scene to facilitate a better understanding of the injury experience of college athletes.

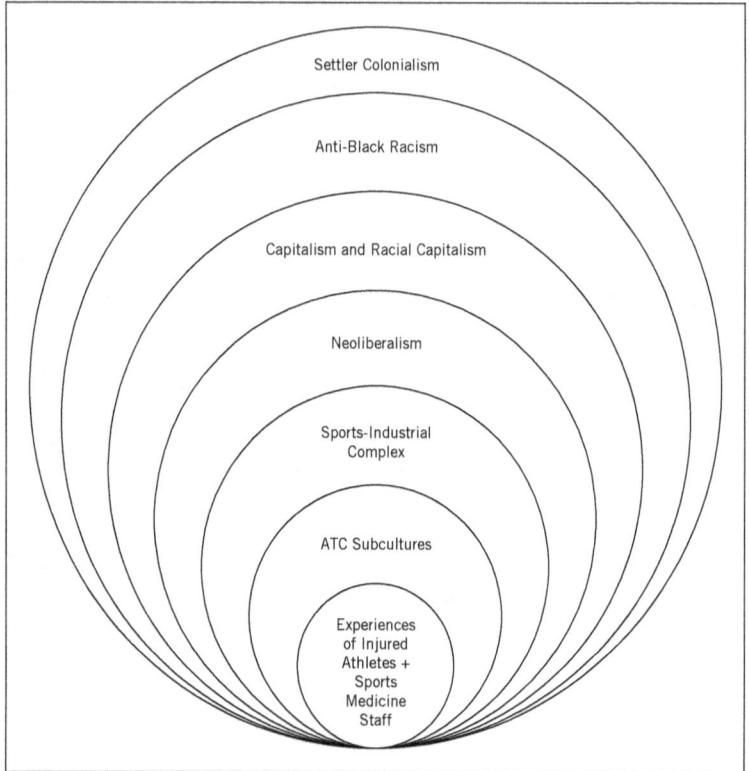

**Figure 0.1** Injured athletes and sports medicine staff location within society.

## The Role of Neoliberalism in College Athletics and Higher Education

The model of neoliberalism affects sport, medical, and academic institutions. One sport institution—the NCAA, originally called the Intercollegiate Athletic Association of the United States—was founded in 1906 (NCAA 2022) in response to concerns expressed by President Theodore "Teddy" Roosevelt and college administrators about the numerous injuries and fatalities occurring in the then new college sport of American football (Ibrahim 1975).

Today, the NCAA (2024c) regulates not only roughly eleven hundred member institutions, with a majority being located in the continental United States, but also institutions in Hawaii, Puerto Rico, and Canada. These academic institutions, specifically, higher education institutions (HEIs), are manifestations of neoliberalism. In her book *University, Inc.*, Jennifer Washburn (2006) posits that universities have turned into corporations, attempting to build their brand to sell to students (who are the consumers). Students pick universities based on criteria such as perceived academic excellence, athletics, and cost of admission. The sociologist Rick Eckstein (2017: 54) observes that "the modern neoliberal university's branding strategies are increasingly focused on intercollegiate athletics." Athletics serve to sustain a university's branding to potential students, whether that is the excellence of profit-generating programs that students can enjoy rooting for or the market signaling of other more niche sports. The historian Henry Heller (2016) contends in his book *The Capitalist University* that in the university setting, learning has been commodified, devaluing education. Academic institutions become corporate entities. Moreover, the kinesiologist Ryan King-White (2018: 13) argues that "NCAA institutions actively seek to undermine the education and autonomy of student-athletes while propagating the notion that the institutions are providing those very things." The scholar Jennifer Hoffman (2020) discusses in her book, *College Sports and Institutional Values in Competition*, how there are institutional tensions between academics and athletics over market pressures. These tensions in mission lead athletes in big-time sports to be treated inequitably, among themselves and among other students, which goes against the purpose of higher education.

In another interpretation the economist James Koch (1973) argues that the NCAA is a cartel, and through this cartel, athletes are recruited by "university-firms," or HEIs, to compete in intercollegiate athletics. College athletes' athletic labor is then being used by intercollegiate athletic departments and HEIs and exploited to bring in more consumers, which are the fans (including students). As part of this function, intercollegiate athletic departments make HEIs more visible to the public (Shulman and Bowen 2001) while serving as the "front porch" for the whole university (Bass, Schaeperkoetter, and Bunds 2015).

The NCAA is part of what the sociologist Joseph Maguire (2005) calls the sports-industrial complex, which runs on a logic of neoliberalism. Within this complex, capitalist pursuits take the lead instead of the health of athlete bodies or the development of the "student-athlete" as a person. The NCAA (2023b) states:

> As a nonprofit organization, the NCAA puts its money where its mission is: equipping student-athletes to succeed on the playing field, in the classroom and throughout life.

However, the sociologist George Sage and colleagues D. Stanley Eitzen and Becky Beal (2019: 9) argue that "a competitive free enterprise system creates winners and losers." So, while the NCAA says that it is trying to make athletes successful in athletics, academics, and life, not all can be successful given the market-like structure of neoliberalism. This is particularly true of college sport, which the higher education scholar Joy Gaston Gayles and colleagues (2018) argue is a result of the neoliberal logic of capitalism. This structure has negative consequences for athletes since the market interest of college sport is making a profit. Athlete care can be useful to maintaining a competitive program, but, because it costs resources and the athlete's well-being only serves the university's profit-generating mission for the limited time they are able to compete in uniform, the university distributes those resources strategically according to market logics. Richard Southall, Crystal Southall, and Brendan Dwyer (2009) draw on the sociologists Roger Friedland and Robert Alford's (1991) theory of institutional logics to examine the consequences of commercialized institutional logics in big-time college sport. One of the commercialized institutional logics they identify—market capitalism—is driven by the mantras of privatization and profit generation, which follows the model of neoliberalism.

The NCAA has instilled a plethora of rules (or bylaws) to aid in their market logics, one of which is amateurism. The *NCAA DI Manual* (2024: xii) states that "member institutions shall conduct their athletics programs for students who choose to participate in intercollegiate athletics as part of their educational experience and in accordance with NCAA bylaws, thus maintaining a line of demarcation between student-athletes who participate in the Collegiate Model and athletes competing in the professional model." The point of this bylaw is for athletes to not be seen as professionals and, therefore, not be entitled to monetary compensation. This model of amateurism follows a view of the value of sports taken from the British upper class (Wheeler 2004; Hextrum 2020a), who engaged in sport for recreation and did not need monetary compensation. Even the term "student-athlete" has a history leading to the institutional logics of capitalism. This term was created by Walter Byers (1995) and the NCAA to signify that athletes are students first and athletes second, not allowing them to be compensated for their labor from which the university profits. The sport scholars Ellen Staurowsky and Allen L. Sack (1998, 2005) urge us to reconsider the term "student-athlete" and the myth that is amateurism.

In this neoliberal model of the university, at an organizational level, the commodification of the athlete body is put before the health of the athlete. While the HEIs of the NCAA may promote social progressivism in certain aspects of their branding and education product, its neoliberal orientation follows an economically conservative model to thrive in the marketplace. So, while the university is soft on social issues, there is still a free market economy at play that uses rather than serves the athletes receiving care.

The logics of neoliberalism mesh well with the cultural idea that sport is a meritocracy—success depends on ability and effort (Dixon 2021). However, higher education scholar Kirsten Hextrum (2021: 7) argues that athletic merit in sport is not a meritocracy but rather "a cultural construct that varies across time, place, and sport." This reveals the "dark side" of sport—the role of neoliberalism—which is what the sociologist Jay Coakley (2015) calls the "Great Sport Myth" (GSM). The GSM challenges the assumption that sport is "pure and good" by virtue of its contribution to personal development through competition. Coakley points out that people often believe that the purity and goodness of sport is transferred to anyone who plays, consumes, or sponsors sport but argues that this belief is a myth. Rather, neoliberal capitalism shapes the sporting machine such that it serves several stakeholders' ends apart from personal development. In his book *Game Over*, the sportswriter Dave Zirin (2011: 107) writes, "Welcome to the NCAA in the twenty-first century, about as corrupt and mangled an institution as exists on the sports landscape."

The private actors, the university and the NCAA (under the guise of privatization—one of the mantras of neoliberalism), in making money by exploiting the ambitions, self-image, hard work, and enjoyment of participants and spectators do so through another mechanism that grew alongside capitalism—exploitation based on racialization and gender discrimination. These lenses influence the ways that athletes, fans, and staff think both about the value of athletic achievement and about how to weigh the power and responsibility of the institution against that of the individual athlete. The structural injustices that are experienced by athletes in the ATC then stem from social constructs built to support settler colonialism and racial capitalism, which are structures that allow neoliberalism to thrive.

## The Roots of Racial Capital, Racialization, and Gender Discrimination

For universities with top athletic programs, sport is a commercial endeavor that supports the financial viability of the university as a whole. Athletes participate in pursuit of their own goals, but both their labor and their bodies are used by the university for its own strategic ends. Profit-generating sports, particularly men's football and basketball, may earn the university ticket sales, television rights, enrollment by students who want to participate in the team's fandom, and name recognition in the markets from which the university recruits students. Even sports programs that do not directly bring in money from spectators—such as crew—contribute to the marketing of the university, its prestige, and its profile in the communities from which the university wishes to draw students. They also help the university construct a concept of the "student-athlete" who, however worthy of care, is allowed to play as a privilege the university grants, not as a labor from which the university benefits. That construction and its implications become more challenging to apply to profit-generating athletes when one contextualizes the differential treatments of profit generating and other athletes in the history of the racialized and gendered bodies in American capitalism.

The American university today operates within an economic system of capitalism, which itself is an outgrowth of settler colonialism. As the philosopher and economist Karl Marx (1844) explained, capitalism is much more than an economic system; it is also a system of power, or a mode of exercising power, where political power has been transformed into economic relations. While an economy seems to those within it to be natural, there are social and political decisions that drive it. This idea of the system being natural is what philosopher Antonio Gramsci (1995) refers to as hegemony.

The current system exists because the rise of capitalism globally encouraged Europeans to look for new economic partnerships (Desmond and Emirbayer 2020). The Spanish were the first to colonize the Americas, looking for economic gain, particularly in gold and silver, in addition to attempting to convert the Indigenous population to Catholicism. Conquistadors, Spanish soldiers, were permitted by the Spanish monarch to seize the land and riches of the New World (i.e., parts of present-day North America, including Florida and the American Southwest, Latin America, and the Caribbean). Later settlers colonized the Americas through Indigenous genocide, land theft—a crucial part of settler colonialism—the enslavement of folk of African descent, and exploitation (Zinn 1980) and, subsequently, formed the United States, a settler state whose establishment was dependent on violence and genocide (Dunbar-Ortiz 2014).

The early capitalist economy relied both on the bodies of exploitable Indigenous folk and on indentured servitude (a status in which laborers are tied to their owner for a fixed amount of time until they are freed). Indentured servants included Indigenous peoples whose land their employers occupied, Africans brought through the Atlantic slave trade, and seventeenth-century Irish.

Settler colonialism includes a racial component, operating often through processes of racialization, that is, when a dominant group attaches racial meaning to a previously unclassified group (Omi and Winant 2015). Racialization labels particular groups superior and other groups inferior, creating a hierarchy of race that continues to guide assumptions about organizational operations today, as is explored in these pages.

While decolonization has occurred, this has not destroyed the power structures of colonialism because the economic system that structured eighteenth-century society continues. Slave labor, referred to by Marx as primitive accumulation of capital (Marx 1867), was not only a source of the American nation's original capital but continues to drive further accumulation today in novel forms of unpaid labor.

Black bodies were historically trafficked as valuable commodities. And, in addition to stealing individuals' capital and labor, the slave trade constructed Africans in the minds of capitalists as inferior and exploitable (Rodney 1972), a construction that continues to frame how Black labor and bodies are understood in the capitalist context of high-level university athletics.

The theorist Jean-Marie Brohm (1978) provides a Marxist critique of sport in his book *Sport: A Prison of Measured Time* and argues that sport reflects capitalist categories where spectator sport is a commodity sold in a capitalist fashion, reproducing class inequalities. Brohm (1978: 47) states, "Bourgeois sport is a class institution, totally integrated into a framework of capitalist production relations and class relations." Examples of this are the NCAA profit-generating spectator sports of football, basketball, and baseball. In these instances, profit-generating sport athletes are the commodities that are bought and sold. In these sports, Black men and women are overrepresented.

The NCAA (2024b) reported that during the 2023 season of men's DI basketball, of the athletes, 24 percent were white, 54 percent were Black, and 22 percent were Other. For men's DI football athletes, 36 percent were white, 48 percent were Black, and 16 percent were Other. For men's DI baseball athletes, 75 percent were white, 6 percent were Black, and 19 percent were Other. For women's DI basketball, 32 percent were white, 42 percent were Black, and 26 percent were Other.

The exploitation of Black athletes can be further understood through the lens of critical race theory (CRT)—a movement by activists and scholars that took root in the 1970s to chart and change the relationship between race, racism, and power (Delgado and Stefancic 2017). CRT centers on U.S. law and questions the foundations of the liberal order (Matsuda et al. 1993). Utilizing one of the tenets of CRT, there are differences in how groups are racialized over time, which is tied to the needs of the labor market. Currently, the majority of NCAA profit-generating athletes who are commodified in profit-generating sports are Black. This changed from the original demographics of college football athletes, the majority of whom were white (Sage, Eitzen, and Beal 2019). When exploitation became necessary to make a profit (which is how capitalism thrives), the market was oriented toward the exploitable, Black men.

The sociology of sport pioneer Harry Edwards (1969) discusses the "Black amateur athletic machine" in his revolutionary work, *The Revolt of the Black Athlete*, which highlights the labored experiences of Black athletes and how their bodies are racialized.[2] Edwards (1969: 16) writes, "Like a piece of equipment, the Black athlete is used." This is particularly the case of Black men in profit-generating sports such as football and basketball. Men in profit-generating sports are both disproportionately Black and often valued simply for what their bodies can do, therefore, they are commodified. Thus, the NCAA, a capitalist enterprise, operates in a racialized way, using profit-generating sport athlete bodies, a majority of whom are nonwhite, to make money for the university.

The late political scientist Cedric Robinson (1983) extended Marx's theory and introduced the concept of racial capitalism to facilitate the understanding of how capitalism operates in a racist system. Robinson argues that racial capitalism *is* capitalism and vice versa. In other words, capitalism depends on racial order and hierarchy and is inherently racialized. Racial domination and inequality have always been core features of capitalism (Gilmore 2017), making racialization and capitalism inseparable from each other (Melamed 2015). This system is detrimental to bodies racialized as exploitable, including those of college athletes.

Capitalism requires inequality for the creation of value, and racism preserves inequality. Robinson's concept of racial capitalism developed from the analysis of apartheid in South Africa in the mid-1970s, a system of segregation and discrimination based on race. Robinson used this concept as an analytical framework for understanding both the history of modern capitalism and how the apartheid state structured race, class, and the accumulation of capital.

The higher education scholars Ezinne Ofoegbu and Leslie Ekpe (2022) argue that the NCAA is a racial capitalist enterprise. Moreover, college athlete healthcare is a manifestation of modern capitalism in a racialized society. This racialized capitalist system can be seen as

---

2. H. Edwards's (1973) dissertation was published as the first integrated textbook titled *Sociology of Sport*, which focused on the sociological analysis of the institution of sport.

operating in the NCAA and collegiate athletics by the way the NCAA and universities profit from the majority Black labor of profit-generating sport athletes.

The journalist William Rhoden (2006) writes in his book, *Forty Million Dollar Slaves*, that while sport organizations profit from Black athletes' labor, these athletes hold little to no power. Rather, Black athletes are exploited in the college sport space. Moreover, the scholar Billy Hawkins (2010) argues that predominantly white institutions (PWIs) shape college sport into what he calls the new plantation. Even Byers, the first executive director of the NCAA, argues in his book with Charles Hammer, *Unsportsmanlike Conduct* (1995: 391), both that there is a "plantation mentality" that exists on university campuses and in the NCAA and that those who benefit from this perspective are the supervisors. In this setting, race as a concept functions to rationalize and justify behavior (Du Bois [1903] 1989). The meaning people collectively—and organizationally—ascribe to racial categories is what gives the concepts power.

Harvey (2005) argues that within neoliberalism, there is a utilitarian justification (many vs. few) that focuses on the consequences rather than the intent behind the behavior. We see this logic applied to how ATC staff weigh their responsibilities. In a chapter in *The NCAA and the Exploitation of College Profit Athletes*, the critical sport scholar Southall (2023) argues that one of these utilitarian justifications is that only a "small" percentage of athletes—profit-generating Black men athletes—are being exploited. We see athletes in the ATC argue over whether the organizational attention on this small segment of athletes is a privilege or a burden. Following this observation, education scholar Albert Bimper (2020), also a former professional football athlete, argues that the neoliberal model perpetuates racial inequality in the U.S. collegiate sport system.

Colonizers also brought patriarchal ideas to the Americas, including constructed meanings of gender. Today, these patriarchal ideologies serve as ways of controlling and extracting cooperation from profit-generating sport athletes who are majority men, the frontline laborers. We see how athletes who are men are conscripted to sacrifice their well-being and comfort for the good of the program with appeals to manliness while athletes who are women feel their gender in the way their concerns and voices are sidelined.

These observations build on the work of Hextrum (2020b), who argues that racist and sexist ideologies persist in college sport. Conceptualizing race and gender as ideologies leads to the recognition that where sexism and racism exist, there is a need for rationalization to justify beliefs (Weber [1904] 1958).

The previously mentioned history has profound implications for understanding the functioning of both the university institution and profit generation, particularly because ideologies of race and gender are embedded in the educational, medical, and sport institutions, which all influence and affect the care college athletes receive. Race and gender protect the meanings these systems rely on to derive value from the products they offer, whether they be entertainment, prestige, experience, or even education. We see processes of racialization and gendering within notions of what value different scholar athletes bring to the athletic product being sold, how their bodies and labor ought to be understood and valued, and what values the university's consumers bring to the transaction. Race and gender shape notions of the ownership the organization—that is, the ATC, the athletic department behind it, and the university behind the department—asserts over athletes' bodies and labor, the way the organization understands the demand for its product, and the ways athletes in the space understand their own bodies and labor relative to those who share the space with them.

## Methods and Case Selection

The arguments I present in this book derive from observations in the ATC, interviews with sports medicine staff members ($n = 18$), and interviews with injured college athletes ($n = 32$). The sample of this study derives from NLU's athletes who experienced injury and the sports medicine staff members who cared for them during the mid-2010s (pre-COVID). There were three related, yet distinct, phases of the study. Phases one and two occurred concurrently. The first phase included observations in the ATC. The reason for the observations of the ATC is two part. First, observations in the ATC allow for an understanding of the knowledge surrounding injury among the sports medicine staff and injured athletes. Second, during observations, rapport is established in the athlete community. Observations in the ATC occurred for three months. I went to the ATC two to three times a week for one to three hours per visit and sixty hours total. While watching rehabilitation sessions, I would ask questions of both the athletes and the sports medicine staff.

The second phase of the study included eighteen unstructured interviews with sports medicine staff. The unstructured interviews focused on the knowledge the sports medicine staff have surrounding injury within the ATC. This phase highlighted the perspective of the sports medicine staff, their world, and the services they provide.

The third, and final, phase of the study consisted of semi structured interviews with athletes who utilize the ATC for an injury. For this study, athletes fit the criteria if an injury occurred as a result of their participation in a sport competition, they sought medical attention within the ATC, and the athlete is currently utilizing resources in the ATC for the injury.

According to the philosopher Hans-Georg Gadamer (1996), meaning emerges from dialogue; therefore, the goal of these interviews was to have a dialogue with the athletes and sports medicine staff members and have them explain, in detail, how they are constructing varying aspects of the ATC. See Appendix 1 for more details on the theoretical framework that guided the methods of this study.

Because I argue the scenes described in this book are animated by racial, gender, and colonial dynamics, and I want the reader to be sensitive to how these power the interactions and conversations I describe, throughout this book, I identify the demographics of the speakers I observed: their gender, racialized identity, and sport or staff position. If the speaker is born outside the United States and, therefore, their nation of origin might also play into the power dynamics being asserted, I note their "international" status as well. Readers can find a list of the people described in the book in Appendix 2.

## NLU

The ATC in this study is housed in NLU, which is a private medium-sized (less than ten thousand undergraduate and graduate students)

PWI in the South Atlantic division of the United States.[3] In the county that the NLU is in, the majority of the population is Hispanic (69.1 percent).

NLU's athletics is part of the Power Five Conferences. The Power Five refer to the top five conferences in the NCAA, which include the Atlantic Coast Conference (ACC), Big Ten Conference, Big Twelve Conference, Pac-Twelve Conference, and Southeastern Conference (SEC). The teams at this institution competed at the NCAA Division I (DI) level, which is the highest level of college sport in the NCAA. Among NCAA DI football, there are two subdivisions: Football Bowl Subdivision (FBS) and Football Championship Subdivision (FCS). NLU is part of the FBS, which is the highest level of competition in the NCAA, which governs most of college athletics.

## Gap in the Literature

While injury among collegiate athletes has been a concern of the NCAA since its inception, there is little medical sociological research into what injury means to athletes and how organizational meanings interact with athletes' own sense of their goals and value. Additionally, data are practically nonexistent on the meaning of injuries among collegiate athletes within the space of an athletic training room (Walk 2004), which is surprising since institutionalized medicine has long been a topic of discussion within the sociological discipline (Foucault [1963] 1973; Freidson 1970; Goffman 1961; Starr 1982). A thorough examination of an ATC and its involvement in the construction of the meaning of college athlete health, specifically focusing on injury, will help fill this void.

While scholars have argued that the NCAA exploits and commodifies the bodies of college athletes (Bimper 2020; Byers and Hammer 1995; H. Edwards 1969; Hawkins 2010; King-White 2018; Ofoegbu and Ekpe 2022; Rhoden 2006; Southall 2023; Zirin 2011), little research has examined the organizational constraints of sports medicine. Therefore, focusing on the inner workings of the ATC, this study utilizes

---

3. The South Atlantic region of the United States includes the District of Columbia and the following states: Delaware, Florida, Georgia, Maryland, North Carolina, South Carolina, Virginia, and West Virginia (U.S. Census 2020).

interpretive methods to identify the "stock of knowledge" that surrounds injury from the perspectives of both the injured collegiate athletes and the sports medicine staff (i.e., athletics trainers, physical therapists, nutritionists, and sport psychologists). In this book, the following questions are examined:

- In the context of the ATC, what is the meaning of injury to collegiate athletes and sports medicine staff?
- What role does NLU play in athlete healthcare and the meaning of injury?
- How does the implementation of athlete healthcare differ for athletes by sport, race, nationality, and gender in the ATC?
- What role do sports medicine staff members play in promoting the neoliberal model in athlete healthcare?

## Organization of the Book

All chapters draw on observations and on interviews with injured athletes and sports medicine staff members. Chapter 1 outlines, broadly, the organization of college athlete healthcare. Chapter 2 provides an overview of the organization of the ATC, which is a bureaucratic organization whose goals include maintaining the power to generate a profit. Chapters 3 and 4 focus on some consequences of the organization of the ATC as a neoliberal bureaucratic organization, such as "in-house" care (Chapter 3) and "sense-making" that occurs amid the contested terrain created (Chapter 4). Chapters 5–7 dive deeper into the inner workings of the ATC and issues pertaining to the racialized (Chapter 5), gendered (Chapter 6), and intersectional inequalities (Chapter 7) constructed and preserved in an organization that operates in a capitalist society. Moreover, these chapters highlight the mechanisms used to reinforce whiteness and masculinity and its effects on athletes and sports medicine staff members. Chapters 8–10 investigate the experiences of injured athletes and the effect these injuries have on their sense of self, or biographies, regarding the recognition of injury (Chapter 8), the uncertainty of injury (Chapter 9), and mobilizing resources to receive care for an injury (Chapter 10). The Conclusion of this book discusses the larger implications of the study for the NCAA, sports medicine (including athletic training) as a discipline, and college athletes.

## Conclusions

The ATC follows college sports' organizational orientation of preserving the commodification of the athlete body in the sports-industrial complex before the health of the athlete at an organizational level. The neoliberal model in place uses dominant ideologies of race and gender that contrast with the stated tenets of the system.

This book analyzes data through the theory of neoliberalism to highlight that college athlete healthcare in ATCs is guided by profit generation and has a contested nature given the historical process of settler colonialism and racial capitalism (which are embedded with dominant ideologies of whiteness and masculinity/paternalism following the social construction of race and gender) that have created this structure of inequality and considers how these structures allow neoliberalism to have a logic to exploit in this contested terrain.

The contested terrain then is the friction between the various actors within higher education and how much power and influence sports medicine staff members should have versus athletes. This battle is a contested terrain that is all within the neoliberal framework. The priority is given to those who meet the goals of neoliberalism—generating a profit.

# 1

## College Athlete Healthcare

Eli, a white men's football athlete, uses his one forearm crutch to slowly reach the athletic training table. Using his arms and one leg, he maneuvers himself onto the table, sitting down with his right leg straight and left knee bent. Eli is wearing shorts with the NLU football logo, and his knee is exposed. His knee looks raw, it is mostly bright red with some patches of black and blue. Eli recently tore his anterior cruciate ligament (ACL) at an away game on what he refers to as "cut up" turf. Within the week, Eli underwent surgery. ACL reconstruction surgery has evolved tremendously over the decades (Chambat et al. 2013) allowing patients to recover faster than ever before. This change has been a boon to the ATC under the neoliberal model of profit generation and with the need both to get athletes back on the field faster than ever before and to optimize the body for profit. Using advances in surgery such as this aids in the institution's end goal of making profit.

Since Eli's surgery, sports medicine staff in the ATC have been working with him diligently. Tom, a white Latino man physical therapist, and Noah, a white man athletic trainer, both employed at NLU walk over to Eli. Tom carefully puts on a pair of blue medical gloves and sits down on the stool in front of the training table and begins to examine Eli's knee. "One, two, three..." he says as he counts the stitches in Eli's knee. Tom pauses and walks a few steps away, quietly consulting Noah. They both walk back, and Noah sits down on the stool in front of Eli. With his glasses on the tip of his nose, he moves closer to Eli's knee to examine it. "Do you want a pair of gloves?" asks Tom. Noah shakes him away with his hand, as if to say no.

Noah grabs a pair of scissors that are on the table next to him and starts to take out the stitches. He begins the process at 8:50 A.M. Eli looks at his knee quickly before lying back on the bench and closing his eyes. Each time Noah touches the scissors to his skin, Eli winces, teeth clenched, eyes shut tight.

Noah begins to narrate his actions, ignoring Eli's alarm, "You want to cut the stitch at the tip of the triangle." Eli sits up halfway and looks at me pleadingly with wide eyes before lying back down again. After a few minutes, with one stitch left, Eli sits up to watch. Noah points to a part of Eli's knee close to the stitches and asks, "Is this a stitch?" "No," says Tom, "it's a scab." At 8:58 A.M., Noah announces, "All done," throwing his hands up in the air.

Tom grabs a swab and cleans the wound on Eli's knee. Noah has gone back to his office at this point. "Do you want STIM?" asks Tom. Eli says no. "What about ice?" asks Tom. "No, I don't like ice. I don't think it works," says Eli, smiling. Tom laughs and walks away. Eli turns to me and says that ice makes his knee stiff, so he doesn't like it. He puts his shoes on to leave, trying to grab his forearm crutch that is just out of reach. I walk over and pick up his forearm crutch and hand it to him. "Thanks, have a good day," says Eli. "You too," I respond. It's the only direct response Eli's received to his words, as opposed to just his body, throughout the interaction.

## Sports Medicine (and Athletic Training)

The NCAA is part of the sports-industrial complex. According to Maguire (2005), there are four institutional elements of the sports-industrial complex: (1) sports medicine, (2) sports science, (3) sports science support programs, and (4) regional/national centers of excellence. While the NCAA originated to track injuries, this function has been deregulated and delegated to sports medicine staff members, who, while working under guidelines adopted by the NCAA, must be licensed through various other governing bodies. One governing body is the American College of Sports Medicine (ACSM 2023) which is an organization whose mission is to "advance and integrate scientific educational and practical applications of exercise science and sports medicine." The sports medicine scholar Jack W. Berryman's (1995) book *Out of Many, One* details the history of the ACSM, which was founded in 1954, originally under the name, "Federation of Sportsmedicine," by eleven individuals. Of the eleven, there were seven male physical educators, one female physical educator, and three male physicians (who were cardiologists). During this time, physicians in the United States acted as team surgeons for institutions with intercollegiate sport, assisted by athletic trainers who were known as "rubbers." In addition to physicians and athletic trainers, ACSM membership is open to any who have a role in the fields of sports medicine and exercise science.

Athletic trainers must also be licensed through the National Athletic Training Association (NATA), pass the Board of Certification exam (BOC), and engage in continuing education unit (CEU) requirements through the Commission on Accreditation of Athletic Training Education (CAATE). The CAATE (2023) is an organization that provides accreditation standards for the athletic training profession.

Athletic trainers began to organize themselves in 1938 (Berryman 1995), forming the NATA. According to the NATA (2021), athletic training "encompasses the prevention, examination, diagnosis, treatment and rehabilitation of emergent, acute or chronic injuries and medical conditions." Within the field of athletic training there are athletic trainers who are "highly qualified, multi-skilled health care professionals who render service or treatment, under the direction of or in collaboration with a physician, in accordance with their education, training and the state's statutes, rules and regulations" (NATA 2021).

In-depth histories of athletic training as a discipline have been produced by the athletic trainers Matt Webber (2013) and Jim Mackie (2019), while Keith Gorse, Francis Feld, and Robert Blanc (2017) have published experiences of practitioners in athletic training rooms at various levels of sport. However, there are few critical analyses of the athletic training room as a space within college sport that influences the experience of college athletes.

Athletic training as a profession began in the United States in the university setting in 1881 (Webber 2013). Colleges and universities in the United States were established during the seventeenth century with Harvard University, the oldest university in the United States, being founded in 1636 with the primary purpose of preparing men for clergy and ministry as religious leaders (President and Fellows of Harvard College 2023), teaching men how to be "good" workers. Over two hundred years later, in 1837, the first historically Black college was established (Oachs 2016). The origin of college sport traces to an 1852 rowing match between students from Harvard and students from Yale (Sage, Eitzen, and Beal 2019). American football developed soon thereafter as a sport mainly for the upper class (Sage, Eitzen, and Beal 2019).

Cognizant of the history of athletic training, and sports medicine broadly, one can discern how this discipline has emerged in parallel with the racialized and gendered universities, athletic departments, and healthcare industry. In the medical care system, the meaning of health is racialized. In their book *Unequal Treatment*, scholars Brian Smedley, Adrienne Stith, and Alan Nelson (2003) examine racial and ethnic disparities that occur in healthcare settings and their roots in both historical and modern inequities. In *Medicalizing Blackness*, the historian Rana Hogarth (2017) argues that medical practitioners in the Atlantic World (1780–1840) used medicine to justify racial differences. These practitioners created and tested ideas about race on slaves, which, in turn, reified Blackness in medical discourse. In her book *Medical Apartheid*, Harriet Washington (2006) discusses the history of medical experimentation on African Americans in the United States. Dominant ideologies of whiteness affect how people of color receive care.

## NCAA "Oversight" of College Athlete Healthcare

The NCAA utilizes a "hands off" approach to college athlete healthcare and has minimal oversight of ATCs. The majority of the responsibility is retained by the NCAA member institutions, the universities. The NCAA (2017) states that each institution should have an athletics healthcare administrator to "oversee" (more on this term in Chapter 6) the institution's athletic healthcare administration and delivery.

To aid the person in this position, the NCAA published the *Athletics Healthcare Administrator Handbook: A Guide for Designated Athletics Healthcare Administrators* to "help [the athletics healthcare administrator] understand and excel in your role, and maximize your contribution to an environment that promotes health and wellness and delivers quality medical care, which serves as the foundation of student-athlete health and well-being" (NCAA 2017: 4). In this handbook, the athletics healthcare administrator is a designated individual at each NCAA member institution. This position is mandated by the NCAA Independent Medical Care legislation which, in the *NCAA DI 2023-2024 Manual* (2023a: 371), states, "An active member institution shall establish an administrative structure that provides independent medical care and affirms the unchallengeable autonomous authority of primary athletics health care providers (team physicians and athletic trainers) to determine medical management and return-to-play decisions related to student-athletes. An active institution shall designate an athletics health care administrator to oversee the institution's athletic health care administration and delivery."

In other words, healthcare in ATCs is not regulated by the NCAA, which is a clear example of one of the tenets of neoliberalism—deregulation. When there is no regulation on how athletes (workers) should be treated, it is easier to exploit workers because the institutions then have the power to decide how care should be apportioned and for whose benefit.

The other incentive of this mode of deregulation is that it takes pressure off of the NCAA. Depending on the mode of delivery, though, there are other actors that could be at risk. There are three models of delivery for college athlete healthcare: the athletics model, the academic model, and the medical model. The biggest difference in these models is to whom sports medicine members report. NLU has a medical model, which means the head athletic trainer reports to the team physician, while all other athletic trainers report to the head athletic trainer. The medical model is endorsed by the NCAA and holds the least legal risk according to scholars Geoffrey Rapp and Christopher Ingersoll (2019). Placing a doctor in charge of medical decisions would seem to minimize harm, depending on the goals of the doctor. But does the doctor look out for the ideal medical outcome for patients or the one that best serves the organizational orientations and their cultural authority?

In the conversations I had with sports medicine staff members, I found that they still expressed fear of legal retaliation. An athletic trainer named David, a Black man, states:

> [Being an athletic trainer] on football there is a fear of getting sued. You worry sometimes. But you have in the back of your mind of like, oh crap... That's why you document everything to make sure that if it ever does hit that situation, you have things to back you up, I did everything that I could in this situation.

Trainers have their potential harm in mind as they practice and build in mechanisms to protect the organization from the repercussions.

While the NCAA (2023a) considers team physicians *and* athletic trainers to be the primary athletics healthcare providers, I found that athletic trainers are truly the primary sports medicine staff members. Athletic trainers categorized themselves as "jacks of all trades," "cruise directors," "liaisons," "middleman/middleperson," "first responders," and "gatekeepers." Each of these terms highlights that athletic trainers are expected to perform a plethora of administrative tasks in addition to making sure athletes are receiving the best care possible. However, athletic trainers work under the direction of team physicians. Due to this arrangement, athletic trainers are pulled in two directions. That is, they are tasked with defining and treating injuries and reporting these problems to the team doctors. And, at the same time, they work closely with the injured athletes and develop close relationships with them, thus serving as a support system.

Based on the informal interactions I observed during my research with sports medicine staff members, it appears that there are times when the team doctors, ostensibly those charged with keeping the care oriented toward good medical outcomes, do not even see the injured athletes but only discuss an athlete's injury with the athletic trainer. Tom explained that sports medicine staff members use a variety of communication methods ranging from telehealth (e.g., SirenMD, Next) to injury reports (i.e., Word documents), to an electronic medical record database system (e.g., Blue Ocean), to in person and phone conversations. When athletic trainers or physical therapists communicate through telehealth with administrative sports medicine staff members, there are instances when the sports medicine staff member is relaying information to the athlete from the administrative sports medicine staff member. The resources are apportioned to allow medical doctors to handle a volume of care efficiently, but not necessarily for personalized attention. Given this structure, the objectification of the athlete body is a regular occurrence.

According to the NCAA (2017: 16), there are numerous key "stakeholders" who may engage with the athletics healthcare administrator: alcohol and drug prevention coordinator, director of academic support, director of athletics, director of counseling/psychological services, director of health services, drug testing site coordinator, faculty athletics representative, head athletic trainer, head sport coaches, head team physician, institutional risk manager, licensed mental health professional, life skills administrator, office for institutional equity, senior compliance administrator, senior woman administrator (SWA), sports dietitian/nutritionist, strength and conditioning coaches, and Title IX coordinator.

Not included in this list of stakeholders in healthcare are the collegiate athletes whose health is the supposed concern of these professionals. So, while there is deregulation in athlete healthcare, the athletes themselves who are receiving this care have no say.

## Health Insurance

The athletic trainer Nancy, a white woman, unwraps the top of her Quest protein bar and takes a bite. With a mouth full of food, she announces, "I just saved you and [NLU] a ton of money, you should tell your superior to pay for my traffic violation." "How?" asks her colleague Tom. "By switching to [Blue Cross Blue Shield] for people not even on [NLU] insurance so now it goes through [NLU] *and then* their own insurance," says Nancy proudly as she takes another bite of her protein bar. Her shifting of the financial burdens of care away from the university are in line with its organizational aims toward profit, and she is confident her colleagues will appreciate her work in line with this goal.

There is a loose system of health insurance that college athletes are required to have. The NCAA (2023c) adopted a "Student-Athlete Medical Insurance Legislation" policy that requires institutions to certify that athletes have insurance coverage. However, this requirement can be achieved in a number of ways. For example, athletes can be covered by their parents' health insurance (e.g., private, state Medicaid, school insurance), by institutional insurance, or by insurance purchased by the athletic department through NCAA distribution funds from an athlete fund. The neoliberal capitalist functioning of athlete healthcare is an extension of the sports-industrial complex; and, in this space, athlete healthcare is privatized.

Like all students, athletes are required to have insurance so they either have their own insurance or insurance through the school. Athletes who do not have their own insurance are required to have insurance through the university. If an athletic injury occurs, then the school insurance will be billed, and the athletic department pays for whatever the school insurance does not cover.

The university acts as a secondary insurer. All students must have their own insurance, including athletes, and then athletes also have insurance through the athletic department. David describes how insurance at NLU works:

> So, how it works is if anybody has an injury or an illness, anything from a papercut up to a surgery, when we take them over to see our doctors, their personal insurance is billed first and then [the athletic department] act as the secondary. We cover the copay, the deductible.

So, an athlete's personal insurance is billed first and then the athletic department. However, the athletic department as a secondary insurer only covers athletic-related injuries. David continues:

> Us, as a secondary, only covers athletically related injuries. So, if a girl happens to get in a car accident, God forbid, they only would get covered by primary insurance. Now, I can help facilitate by helping them see a doctor or, if they're injured, kind of help with the rehab part of it. But the cost that would be incurred would be responsible by the student-athlete, not by us.

If they are walking outside, trip and fall, and hurt their knee, if it didn't occur through something that was athletically related, it would be out of their own expenses.

This raises a concern for those who only have health insurance while they are athletes but suffer injuries that require long-term healthcare. In addition, when the athletic department is the secondary health insurance, it only covers athletic injuries that occurred during sport. So, for example, if an athlete is playing pickup basketball and is injured, it is not covered. This leads to conflicts over whether an injury was incurred as a result of athletics or outside the athlete's official sport activities; the athlete may have to prove their injury is one the athletics program is responsible for if the institution decides to shift blame.

Another concern is when an athlete requires care that the ATC or its insurance does not provide. For example, sport psychologist George, a white man, states:

We always try to do our best to get someone [a healthcare provider] who is under the university insurance, but that is not a requirement. It's nice, but they don't have to be. It's about getting the athlete to the right place.

Unfortunately, the "right place" may not be covered by insurance and cost money that an athlete cannot afford.

## Conclusions

Maguire (2005) argues that the goal of the sports-industrial complex—maximum efficiency in sport—is detrimental to sport, people, and humanity. Since sports medicine staff members are governed by various privatized entities, extensions of neoliberalism, they have had to adapt to the market structure. This affects their ability to provide the best care since there are other concerns, particularly financial considerations, that conflict with athlete care.

# 2

## The Organization of NLU's Athletic Training Center

Sammy, an undergraduate athletic training student and Black woman, walks slowly into the main athletic training room carrying a large cardboard box that is blocking her vision. "WHAT'D WE GET?!" athletic trainer Noah shouts. Sammy places the box down gently, "The carts came in," she replies, and turns around to get another box. "The carts came in time for the special occasion!" says Noah. "What is the special occasion?" asks athletic trainer Nancy. "It's opening day," says Noah, "there are going to be a lot of big names here." "Oh, like people that donated," says Nancy. Minutes later, there are sounds of hammering and clicking as the undergraduate athletic training students assemble the carts. "Sounds like Santa's workshop in here!" shouts Noah.

The donors that Noah is referring to are a major part of NLU athletics and profit in general. At NLU, profit-generating sports (i.e., football, baseball, and basketball) are regarded very highly by stakeholders and the university's branding is centered around these sports. The politics of the university affect the economy of the university, particularly the part people of power play in the distribution of wealth among the university's priorities and marketing. So, while the ATC is a facility where professionals deliver health services to college athletes, there are organizational constraints that affect its priorities, too. Namely, the donors are more likely to give more money to the university if they believe it will benefit the success of those profit-generating sports.

## ATC

Included in the ATC is a web of services that are provided by physicians, athletic trainers (some of whom are graduate students), physical therapists, undergraduate athletic training students, a sport psychologist, and nutritionists. Within the ATC, there is one medical center, three athletic training rooms, a strength and conditioning center, and sport training fields (i.e., grass and turf fields). The medical center houses the team doctors, who are an integral part of the sports medicine community and the organization of the ATC. These doctors are in charge of the care that athletic trainers provide to the athletes.

Of the three athletic training rooms, I refer to one as the "main athletic training room," one as the "baseball athletic training room," and one as the "basketball athletic training room." The main athletic training room houses the majority of the sports teams, including both the profit-generating sport of men's football and all the non-profit-generating sports listed here: women's and men's cross-country, women's swimming and diving, men's diving, women's and men's tennis, women's and men's track-and-field, women's golf, women's rowing, women's soccer, and women's volleyball. Of the other two athletic training rooms, one houses men's baseball and the other men's and women's basketball, all of which are profit-generating sports.

To qualify as a profit-generating sport athlete, the sport must bring profit to the university. For the purposes of this book, profit-generating sports include men's football, men's baseball, men's basketball, and women's basketball (Kidd et al. 2018; Southall et al. 2015). According to Southall and colleagues (2015: 405), "Profit-athletes are NCAA college athletes whose estimated market value exceeds the value of NCAA-approved compensation." When a sport generates profit, the revenues exceed the expenses associated with sponsoring the sport. Profit-generating sports, then, differ from simply revenue-generating sports. The latter are sports that may generate income, but this amount does not exceed the expenses needed to pay the costs of the sport. Many sports generate revenue, but fewer generate a profit. Revenue pays for the expenses of operating the team, such as hiring staff and the purchasing of equipment and supplies. In fact, sports that do not generate a profit depend on resources paid for by the profit-generating programs. (That said, the university and its profit-generating programs benefit from the other athletic programs in other ways.) Thus, revenue drives the operating of the team and the athletic department. Profit then reflects a financial gain after subtracting expenses.

All athletes are exploited in the ATC; however, there are variations. Profit-generating sport athletes are seen as the most valuable commodities in the ATC, compared to non-profit-generating sport athletes. Therefore, the availability of profit-generating sport athletes to play, if able-bodied, receives priority treatment in the ATC. After this priority is accommodated, non-profit-generating athletes then receive care.

This, then, affects how profit-generating athletes are treated. If priority is given to profit-generating sport athletes, then non-profit-generating athletes are not receiving the same level of care. However, regardless of their position, athletes do not have a platform for making decisions about their health or their well-being. If an athlete participates in a profit-generating sport, the institution may fear the athlete choosing their long-term well-being over the success of the program. If an athlete participates in a sport that does not generate a profit, the institution may worry that their needs will detract from the resources available for the profit-generating sport. The sports medicine institution is not designed to care for all injured athletes. It is geared to fix profit-generating sport athletes that can be fixed and to discard those who are broken. If there is another body of an athlete available to use, then the ATC focuses on them.

## The Main Athletic Training Room

Surrounding the perimeter of the main athletic training room are ten sports medicine staff member offices (see Figure 2.1). Each office has a floor-to-ceiling glass window. These windows allow for an unobstructed view of the interior of the room. Within the interior lay twen-

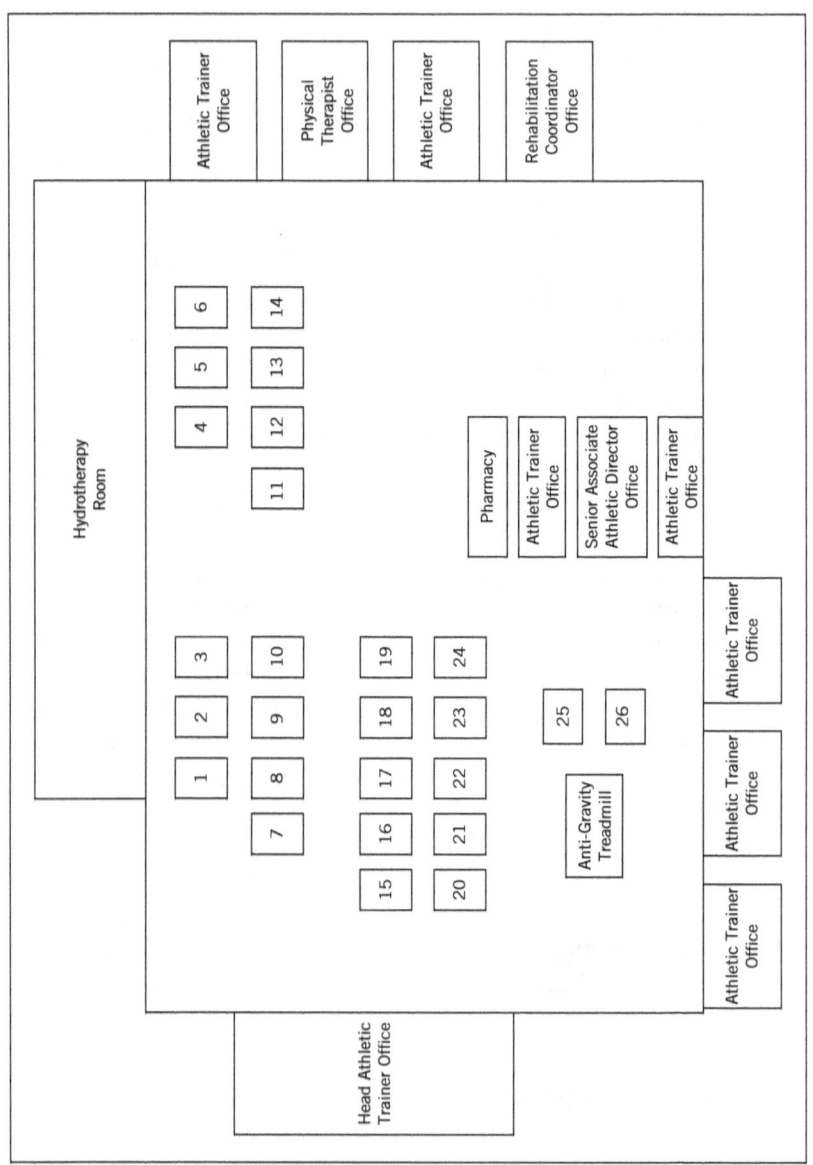

**Figure 2.1** Main athletic training room.

ty-six training tables. These training tables are where athletes receive care from sports medicine staff members.

In the athletic training rooms, the training tables are the most utilized space. Sports medicine staff described these tables as the places where a majority of care is given to athletes. These training tables are used for stretching, flushes (i.e., massages), STIM, blood flow restriction (BFR), ultrasound, Normatec compression therapy, ankle taping, and so on. During an interview with Derek, a white athletic trainer, I ask him what the training room is used for. Derek begins to discuss the training tables and the various services that are provided on them, adding that "the tables are the center of this room. We use them for absolutely everything." This theme was common among sports medicine staff members who often explained the use of the athletic training room by explaining the athletic training tables. While the tables are described as the "center," who is on them matters.

The NLU logo can be seen all over the main athletic training room; embroidered on the athletic training tables and plastered on the walls, the office doors, the floor, and even the garbage cans. The sociologist Samantha King (2012: 77) aptly describes how physical spaces of college campuses (which are corporate universities) have been transformed as brand names and logos are placed in spaces such as the athletic facilities.

Looking around the main athletic training room, I was shocked by the number of services provided. When talking to Katie, a white woman athletic trainer, about all that is available, she responds, "It's a Division I for sure." Katie expressed that this is one of three DI training rooms she has worked in and, surprising to me, the smallest.

The setup of this training room, a panopticon (Foucault [1975] 1977), is a metaphor for the system of power observed in this space. The objects of power on the tables in the center of the room are visible from all angles to the experts wielding power from offices on the outside of the room. Hatteberg (2018) describes a similar setup in her study, where she observed the college athletic center being lined with clear glass windows. She argues that this enabled for visibility and surveillance of athletes. The purpose of this setup is to provide visual access to the laborers (i.e., athletes) who are commodities in this organization.

## Centering of Profit-Generating Sport Athletes

In the main athletic training room, football, the profit-generating sport, is given priority and centered. This prioritization affects the healthcare that these athletes and other athletes in the ATC receive. So, while athletes in non-profit-generating sports are part of the main athletic training room, they lie on the outskirts.

The doctor of physical therapy (DPT) student Elizabeth, a white woman, is conducting an evaluation of Damien, a Black men's track-and-field athlete. Tom, a white Latino physical therapist, tells Damien to lie on his stomach with his hips on the edge of the training table. Tom then tells Damien to lift his trunk up and down in a back extension while Elizabeth holds his legs down. Damien begins to do the back extensions, and Elizabeth has to adjust her stance multiple times to keep Damien stable. Tom asks Damien if it hurts to do this; Damien says no. Tom then tells Damien to get on his knees for Russian hamstring curls (where, on the table, he uses his muscles to slowly lower from a kneeling position until he is on his stomach). Damien begins doing these curls, and Tom critiques him saying that he is bending too much at his butt. Damien adjusts his form and does a few more curls. Tom then asks Damien to get up on his feet and come closer to a wall. The wall is short in width with a television on the same wall. On either side of the wall there are glass windows looking into the pool room. Tom leaves and comes back with a clear goniometer. Tom puts the goniometer on the floor, a few inches from the wall, and asks Damien to stand next to the measuring device and bend his knee to touch the wall. Tom takes a measurement. Tom then asks him to switch feet and takes a measurement of the other knee. Tom says that he is looking for discrepancies between the measurements. Tom walks to put the goniometer away. At that moment, the television that is right above Damien is tuned to an ESPN replay of a recent NLU football game (which took place eleven days prior). The room goes silent as everyone watches intently. "Is this us sucking?" shouts Anne, a white Latina athletic trainer and physical therapist, who is working with a different athlete from the other side of the training room. "Yup," says one of the other trainers. While Damien is in the middle being evaluated—and corrected—football takes over, capturing the attention of all in the room. Football is the center in the main athletic training room, regardless of who is in the athletic training room receiving or providing care.

In the main athletic training room, the structure of the organization and the pressure from NLU to generate a profit causes football to be at the center and other sports to be on the periphery. In an interview with nutritionist Jane, a white woman, she explains one of the benefits of profit-generating sports, outside of receiving attention:

> We have our nutrition center right here, which is essentially our supplemental nutrition resource for all our athletes. And then, some of the other teams whose budget allows for them to have their own fueling station, they have essentially their own little nutrition center in their own locker rooms, or their areas. So, like football has completely their own budget. They have their own dietitian, nutritionist, people over there, and then we are on the Olympic side.

The "Olympic" side she is referring to comprises all the other sports that are part of the main athletic training room, aside from football. While football is the center of the organization, even football athletes have negative experiences, including being objectified. However, football athletes are objectified differently than non-profit-generating sport athletes in this space. Football athletes are the priority; therefore, they are given care first. Sports medicine staff need to treat these athletes as quickly as possible to get them back out on the field, since they are part of a profit-generating sport. Non-profit-generating sports are objectified differently. For these athletes, their bodies are treated as second behind football. These athletes are treated when there is time. In addition, the injuries of athletes from non-profit-generating sports are occasionally contrasted with football injuries in such a way that they appear to be viewed as less significant.

While an important goal of the ATC is to provide the best care for athletes, the unstated goal of the ATC seems to be to maintain power and generate revenue by profiting off of the most valuable commodities (i.e., football, baseball, and men's and women's basketball). In the ATC, then, sports medicine staff are trying to expedite athlete healthcare (e.g., evaluation, diagnosis, prerehabilitation, treatment, rehabilitation, and education) to "fix" these bodies as efficiently as possible to enable their return to participation in sport, unless there are other bodies available. This is, again, due to the way that athlete healthcare is organized around profit-generating bodies.

## Power in the ATC

The ATC is what Weber ([1904] 1958) calls a bureaucratic organization. Bureaucratic organizations operate in a bureaucracy, which is a way of maintaining authority (Lune 2010). The sociologist William Richard Scott (1992) argues that bureaucracies that maintain their authority exhibit the following characteristics: a fixed division of labor, hierarchy of offices, rules that govern performance, separation of personal life from work life, selection of employees based on technical qualifications, and employment viewed by participants as a career. All these characteristics are seen in the ATC.

Bureaucracies function to preserve themselves and those with power. Therefore, if those at a lower level try to dispute or bring up controversial issues, those in power do what they can to preserve the institution no matter the cost.[1] This stability may occur at the expense of the individuals in the institution (i.e., the athletes and athletic staff), whose individual freedom is limited in the bureaucracy. Due to the way bureaucracies are set up, power falls into the hands of a few leaders (Perrow 1972). In this case, power in the ATC is held by the administrative staff. However, most of the administrative staff members spend their time outside of the training rooms (i.e., they are outside of the areas where most of the athlete healthcare is performed).

The imagery of the official organization of the ATC mimics a classic bureaucracy as explained by Scott (1992). First, there is a fixed division of labor that is highly differentiated in terms of the responsibilities that each person shoulders. Second, there is a hierarchy of offices presented with official communication channels. The image is conveyed that all sports medicine staff answer to one member of the administrative sports medicine staff (i.e., the associate athletic director). Third, rules govern performance. Fourth, there is a separation of personal life from work life. Indeed, many sports medicine staff

---

1. In traditional terms, an institution is defined as "any way of organizing relationships that are widely familiar and routinely practiced" (Lune 2010: 2).

reported that they see those in the ATC more frequently than their own families. Fifth, employees are selected based on technical qualifications. To work within the ATC, there are specific qualifications needed for each position. For example, athletic trainers must be certified through the Athletic Training Board of Certification. Sixth, and finally, sports medicine staff view their employment as a career.

On paper, the ATC appears to be bureaucratic, hierarchical, and structural and represents a centered organization (see Figure 2.2). At the center of the ATC is the associate athletic director. In addition to being in charge of all sports medicine staff members, the associate athletic director is the head athletic trainer for the men's football team.

Surrounding the associate athletic director in Figure 2.2 are administrative sports medicine staff members, athletic trainers, and physical therapists. Most of the administrative sports medicine staff members (e.g., senior associate athletic director, deputy athletic director, rehabilitation coordinator, and medical director) are placed above or level with the associate athletic director in the figure. The deviant example of this is the senior associate athletic director who is placed below the associate athletic director. Core and peripheral sports medicine staff members are all placed below the associate athletic director in the figure. Graduate assistant athletic trainers are not connected to the associate athletic director but rather hang at the bottom of the figure. Of the thirteen certified athletic trainers, six are assigned to the men's football team. Note that not listed in this organizational figure are the rest of the physicians (aside from the medical director), the SWA, the sport psychologist, or nutritionists.

The way the organization is portrayed is internalized by those in the organization (e.g., sports medicine staff and athletes). Due to this internalization, sports medicine staff and athletes begin to take for granted certain ways of doing things (Schutz 1970); these ideas are firmly institutionalized (Lune 2010). These behaviors are not ascribed to or dependent on individual choices but rather to the position in the organization, which serves to enact the organizational priorities and the social meanings—the racial, gender, and neoliberal status quo—that animated them. Once behavior becomes institutionalized in an organization, individual members may leave but the way the organization runs will be unchanged because the same procedures are followed by those who remain.

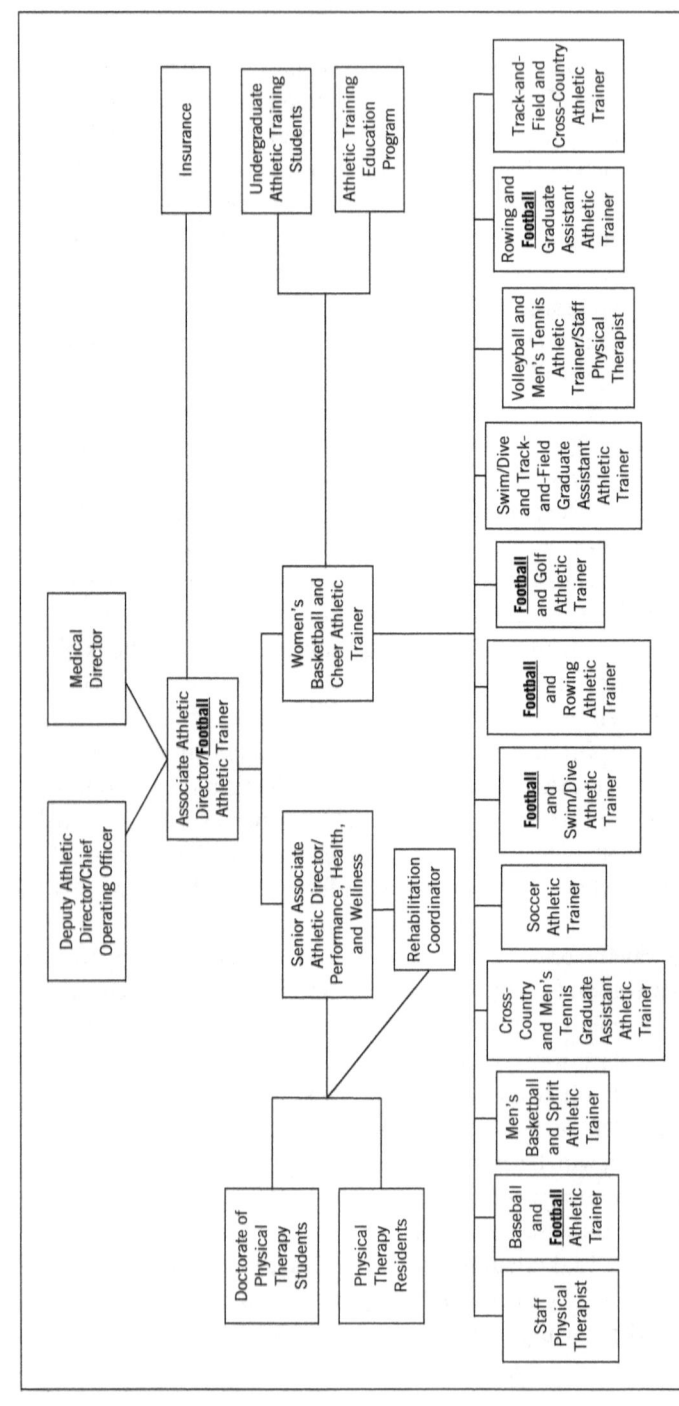

**Figure 2.2** Organizational chart of the athletic training center.

Throughout the years I conducted this study, there was turnover among sports medicine staff in almost every position. However, while the people in the ATC changed, the structure of the organization and the dominant ideals stayed the same. That new people were coming into the ATC did not matter because the structure is constantly being reinforced, resulting in the ATC staying the same. This observation highlights the weight the structure of the ATC has on athlete healthcare.

The ATC, and collegiate athletics, is a cultural world with habits that are ingrained into the consciousness of those who work there. These habits, and consciousness, are then impressed onto athletes who inhabit the ATC. Described more intimately, institutions create meaning, and the components of that arrangement strives to maintain the overall system of meaning.

Weber believed rationalization would lead to an "iron cage" of rationalized systems because this process begins to infiltrate every aspect of life in the organization (Weber [1904] 1958). In this sense, bureaucracy is a method of analysis that can begin to infiltrate organizations because people are led to believe that they are trapped. This feeling of entrapment occurs because of the way the organization is discussed (e.g., the imagery portrayed). To those who work and receive care within the ATC, this organization seems to be real. Therefore, these people live by the rules of the organization.

Organizations are constructed—a facade of people, functions, and policies that can be replaced when a better option is presented, all of which conceals the choices made at the institutional level. People interacting with the organization assume the aspect they are engaging acts on valid knowledge (Toombs 1992). The bureaucracy conceals the operation of power at a high level. When new people are brought into the organization, the people who are currently working and receiving care convey the idea that the ATC is real, giving the impression that newcomers must live by the prevailing rules. This is because of the power dynamic involved in the organization.

While the ATC is presented as a formal organization, this organization actually operates informally. The ATC presents itself as a formal organization to maintain legitimacy within the larger bureaucratic framework where it exists (i.e., sports-industrial complex). So, while the sports-industrial complex provides a broad organizational framework, athlete healthcare issues must be worked out locally (i.e., within the ATC). Weber ([1921] 1978) was interested in structures of authority, one of which he called rational-legal authority. There are many forms to this structure of authority but the purest form to Weber was bureaucracy. He believed that a bureaucracy could attain the highest degree of efficiency of control (Weber [1921] 1978).

Within bureaucratic organizations, formal and informal structures exist. Formal structures have explicitly defined social positions and relationships, while, in informal structures, the positions and characteristics of the participants are difficult to differentiate (Scott 1992).

According to the sociologist Howard Lune (2010: 2), an organization is a group with a name, a purpose, and a defined membership. The organization discussed in this chapter is the ATC. Within an organization, there are clear boundaries between those who are in the organization and those who are not (Lune 2010). The defined membership consists of those positions identified in the organizational chart of the ATC (see Figure 2.2). While large organizations are commonly discussed as bureaucratic, the degree to which smaller organizations are similarly bureaucratic is often overlooked.

## Conclusions

Bureaucratic organizations consist of structures that are centered around power. Since power comes into play, this makes the ATC a space where sense-making occurs, and a contested terrain is created. One way that power operates in this space is by engaging in sense-making and making it a contested terrain.

The ATC is centered around the most valuable commodities, profit-generating sport athletes. The ATC is a controlling organization where an aspect of power comes into play *because there is an organizational context for the way sports medicine staff deal with injury*. According to Weber ([1921] 1978), power is defined as the chance to impose one's will on the behavior of another.

On the other hand, objectification is softened since the ATC operates as an informal structure. This concealment behind informality allows athletes' bodies to be objectified. The next chapter explains the issues that arise from the informal operation of this organization.

# 3

# In-House Care

Noah, Tom, Brian, and Oliver, all men sports medicine staff members, are inside Noah's office with the door closed. I watch intently from outside trying to read Noah's lips as he talks. We make eye contact. He stares at me for a moment before he turns his back toward me. Elizabeth watches this interaction and walks over to me. She tells me that they are talking about a football athlete who wants to see a personal doctor outside of the ATC. I question why this has prompted a closed-door discussion. She explains that sports medicine staff want to keep the care "in-house" because of the logistics surrounding care. While athletes are technically allowed to receive care outside of the ATC, the ATC sports medicine staff members insist that they be allowed to diagnose an athlete to provide care so that the athlete experiences pressure from the organization to help achieve its goals. This tension can be seen in the following example with Brianna, a white women's rowing athlete.

Brianna discusses her experience getting treatment for a sudden pain in her wrist while she is home on break from university. Since she is home, she seeks care from a personal doctor (outside of the ATC) and is diagnosed with a cartilage tear. When she tells sports medicine staff members in the ATC of the outside provider's diagnosis, she is reprimanded for not keeping care in-house. Brianna is then taken to the ATC doctor who tells her that the diagnosis she received from the outside doctor is incorrect and there is nothing wrong with her wrist. However, Brianna continues to experience pain. She complains to various other sports medicine staff members about the pain she is experiencing and is told that she is fine and just needs to rest. After experiencing evasion by sports medicine staff for over a year, she finally undergoes an exploratory procedure so that the ATC doctors can try to determine the source of her pain. The doctors confirm that her pain is in fact coming from a cartilage tear, the same diagnosis she received over a year earlier from her personal provider. It is not until Brianna receives a diagnosis from doctors in the ATC that treatment can begin. Brianna expresses her disdain for having to wait so long (over a year) to get treatment, and states, "I was advocating for myself the entire time and no one in athletics was behind me."

The ATC challenged and undermined Brianna's ability to exercise her own power over her body, preferring that she defer to them as the authority on how best to return her to working order for the athletics program. One could speculate that it may have been to their benefit to keep her able to play rather than undergoing a surgery that would keep her out or they may have preferred to spare the expense for an athlete in a sports program that was not profit generating, but neither explanation is necessary, because the exercise of the organization's authority and the maintenance of its monopoly over knowledge of how to treat injuries is sufficient reason in itself to keep athletes from using outside resources to question the decision-making power of the organization. The organization benefits from the advantages granted to it by systems of race, gender, and economics to nudge athletes toward compliance. In an interview, William, a white staff physician, discusses what he believes the importance of keeping care in-house is. He states, in a paternalistic tone:

> If an athlete chooses to go outside of our system, they have the . . . *I guess* . . . the prerogative to do that. But a couple of things you have to remember. Number one, that may not be covered financially by our system. And number two, most importantly, is we as the team physicians, athletic trainers, physical therapists . . . the entire medical staff, we make the decisions about

return to play because . . . I hate to use the term "liability," but we do assume their care, right? And their abilities to participate and compete. So ultimately, we still have to sign off. We need the student-athletes to understand that ultimately, we make the decisions about playability or not.

This physician points to the medical system that the university requires students to be a part of and to a hazy legal justification as reasons for the athlete to trust them; insurance and law are both institutions that the university is confident are more likely to act in cooperation with its own neoliberal aims than in support of an athlete's individual attempt to exercise self-determination. This example highlights how the ATC uses its bureaucracy according to Weber's vision because the NLU ATC promotes the idea that it is superior to other organizations (e.g., private doctors outside of the ATC). Those who work within these bureaucracies are loyal to these organizations and their goals. This behavior is highlighted by the value placed on in-house care. Throughout the interviews with sports medicine staff, the consensus was that keeping athlete care in-house was best. In-house care refers to receiving assistance solely within the ATC organization. Keeping care in-house allows sports medicine staff to be in control of the space. According to the economist Richard Edwards (1979: 17), control is defined as "the ability of capitalists and/or managers to obtain desired work behavior from workers." In this analogy, capitalists are the sports medicine staff while workers are the athletes. In a more nuanced sense, the capitalists can be seen as the administrative sports medicine staff while the workers are the athletic trainers, physical therapists, and the athletes. And, because of this arrangement, the objectification of both workers and athletes is occurring.

John, a white Latino man who works on staff as a physical therapist, is discussing the resources in the ATC. He mentions an in-house pharmacy in the main athletic training room and states,

> Athletes are given their prescription and at the end of their drug course they give the pills that they have not taken back.

I ask what is done with the medications that are given back. He responds, "They are reused for the next person." Even the medication is kept in-house. This in-house system ensures that the resources apportioned to one athlete are not "wasted" and continue to go to the organization's goals.

Keeping care in-house allows the athlete's body to be further objectified because the athlete is not a subject with power over their own care. There is no room to get a second opinion from sports medicine staff outside of NLU or those who work within the NCAA system. This is not the opinion of one staff member. When asked about getting second opinions from sports medicine staff outside of NLU, James, a white man who works as an athletic trainer responds, "It's a lot better and we try to educate the athlete too that if you keep it all in-house, the communication is better." James continued by explaining, "I think keeping everything in-house is beneficial for [the sports medicine staff members] and for [the athletes]." This sentiment is similar to that expressed by other sports medicine staff members. For example, William, a peripheral sports medicine staff member, states, "Ideally, we would have a full department where we can do a lot of the work in-house." The plan to keep care in-house is another means to an end, specifically to care for athletes as efficiently (with regard to resources needed by the athlete) and with as much control and authority maintained by the organization and its bureaucracy as possible. Although this strategy may be beneficial for the NLU, its athletic department, and the sports medicine staff, keeping care in-house is not necessarily the most beneficial approach for the athlete. This in-house care is another way the body is objectified.

Another important aspect of in-house care is the relationships that are cultivated. Especially important is that the organization is understood in a structural way; therefore, structural inequities are played out in these relationships. The staff expert is acting in their capacity to serve the larger organizational goal, not personally. Moreover, power can be understood as expressed through these relationships.

### The Role of Trust

A common theme revealed in interviews with the sports medicine staff members is the importance of trust in creating strong relationships. Athletes are urged to "trust" or be subservient to sports medicine healthcare providers. Indeed, these healthcare providers may prescribe care without any serious consultation with the athletes. According to William, the linchpin to keeping control in the organization is "trust." William states:

> Once [the athletes] get your trust, it becomes a lot easier. And that's where athletic trainers are invaluable because I think they get their trust quicker because they're there on the field.

William is accurate in the role that athletic trainers play. This is how the levels of organization combine to present a reassuring experience to athletes that obscures the power operating through the levels of bureaucracy—by embedding individual trainers recognizably and visibly in particular programs, who mobilize athletes' trust toward them to enact the goals of the ATC as a whole. James, states:

> It's all about building relationships with these guys and building that trust. I can guarantee you all 35 of my guys, if I told them to go jump off the parking garage, if it would make them better, they would do it because they trust me. I think that is huge in this. If they don't have trust, then this doesn't work. They don't fight me too much because they do trust me. They know I'm going to do the best thing for them.

According to the sociologist Niklas Luhmann (1979: 7), "Trust occurs within a framework of interaction which is influenced by both psychic and social systems, and cannot be exclusively associated with either." Luhmann contends that trust holds organizations together and not simply structures.

Sport psychologist George also discusses the importance of trust, particularly for his role. He states:

> That's part of my job is creating trust. That's why I'm trying to be as visible as possible. Not that being visible equates to trust, but it's one piece of the trust issue.

George explains how he makes a point to walk around the main athletic training room daily so that athletes begin to see him as a familiar face. If he is going to get athletes to talk to him about their mental distress and how to react in a way that serves the program, they need to have a level of trust in him.

Staff physician Catherine, a white woman, also discusses how it is important for athletes to trust sports medicine members. She explains:

> There's a certain amount of buy-in that needs to occur and trust in me that needs to occur. Luckily, my coaches have my back too, so they can kind of help reinforce that trust.

Catherine explains how athletes need to trust her to listen to her about injuries and rehabilitation, but, if there is some level of distrust, she will have a coach step in to reassure that what she is saying is truthful. Thus, the ATC can mobilize another authority figure within the university whom the athlete trusts to reinforce the goals of the ATC, which are those of the athletic program and the university as a whole.

## Consequences of In-House Care

Keeping care in-house also has consequences for sports medicine staff members. The major consequence is that the athletes are uniformly funneled to an overwhelmed and limited staff. Therefore, sports medicine staff members experience a range of issues related to the amount of work but limited staff in this space. The fact that the organization conserves resources to protect its profit, that the university exploits the labor of its athletes, and that athletes are subject to surveillance, exploitation, and control does not mean that ATC staff is not itself overworked and exploited in service of the organization's profit goals as well.

Through observations and interviews with sports medicine staff members, it became apparent that these individuals' caseloads are extremely heavy. Athletic trainers often work six to seven days a week for over twelve hours a day in season. For example, the men's baseball team had only one full-time athletic trainer for thirty-two athletes, while the men's football team had only two full-time athletic trainers for eighty-five athletes.

Athletic trainers often discuss how they saw athletes more than they saw their own families. In my interview with David, he states:

> Basically, wherever they are, I am. Practices, games, I take them to all of their doctors' appointments, I'll drop them off at all their MRI appointments. Pretty much what I tell the parents is that I'm mom and dad away from home, so I see them more than I see my wife.

Similarly, Noah discusses how many hours he works and states:

> I talk to my team doctor more than I talk to my wife. I've been with my team doctor for almost 20 years, so we have a great relationship. So, we talk more, and I update him on everything. My biggest thing with him is try not to give him any surprises.

In addition to being stretched thin, this understaffed ATC devoted a disproportionate share of resources to the football team. This focus on one sport team takes away from other sports, even if a staff member works additionally with a different sport. For example, there are times when an athletic trainer is assigned primarily to a single sport (e.g., men's tennis) but is expected to share time with the football team. In some of these instances, the athletic trainer will be with the football team and will spend time with members of the tennis team if needed.

Noah discusses the importance of getting to know the athletes on the team he is in charge of. He states:

> I do everything the football team does. I go to every team meeting, I go to every function, I'm with the team at the hotel, I'm with the team on the bus, because I want to be around my players as much as I can so I can know my players. And so, when I have a new kid come in, you have 117 different positions, different attitudes, different cultures, so you have to look at each kid differently. Make sure you take care of each one, individually, to the best of your ability. Give them the best healthcare.

This notion of being overworked was common for all sports medicine staff members, even those working with non-profit-generating sport athletes. This burden is even more complicated for athletic trainers who are also still in school. Athletic trainer Joe, an Asian man, explains that his contract states that he works twenty hours; however, in season, he works at least twelve hours (5:00 A.M. to 5:00 P.M.) a day seven days a week, adding up to roughly eighty-four hours a week (which is sixty-four hours more than he is contracted to work). Joe must juggle this time-intensive work schedule while also being a full-time graduate student. Joe's classes are all in the evening. I ask him when he can get schoolwork done, and he responds:

> I try to squeeze some time out of my day to do school stuff. If I have some time here and there. Usually when I come in at five o'clock am, I have a 30 minute to an hour window where I can just do paperwork or work on schoolwork and stuff, or I'll just go home [after work/class] and just shower, eat dinner and then before I go to bed just do work.

While sports medicine staff members are working long hours, they are not being compensated for this "overtime." In an interview, James, explains that he is a salaried employee; therefore, he is not compensated for working more than his allotted hours. I ask him how much he works, and he responds:

> So, every week is different, to be honest with you. If we're home and we don't have a game, I'm usually here from 7am–8pm every day, typical practice day. I also teach at the university, so some days are longer than others. Gameday, I can be here from 9am–11pm. On a Saturday, because we play on weekends, I'm usually here . . . this year we're actually pushing it back. It used to be at 12pm, but now I'm pushing it back to 2pm to try to give all of us, me and [Michael], some to recover, too. So, we'll probably go from 2pm–11pm or 12am, probably.

In addition to this work schedule, James discusses how he has picked up an additional job teaching at the university in the undergraduate athletic training program to make more money due to the high cost of living in the city in which NLU is located. However, some sports medicine staff members can utilize their social and family economic capital to survive in their position. When talking to an athletic trainer named Oliver, a white man, I ask him about his ability to live in the area given his salary. He responds:

> I get help. I get help from my family on some things. I don't want to say they're major things, but they'll be like, "Hey, let me buy your groceries for these couple weeks. Let me pay your car insurance for this month." Something like that. That helps out, goes a long way. But I know there's other people that don't get help. It's hard, it's a struggle for them.

Oliver is right. Interviews with other sports medicine staff members, particularly athletic trainers, reveal that getting help from family or loved ones is not common. Rather, this is a privilege that few staff members have.

## Conclusions

The ATC's policy of encouraging athletes not to seek outside medical attention serves the organization's ability to control care and maintain authority over athletes. It ensures both that decisions made about athlete care be undertaken by professionals with the institution's goals in mind and that the care not use unnecessary resources. Many social advantages help protect the ATC's control. The work of earning athlete trust is labor intensive, and the staff is victim to its own success at convincing athletes to keep care in-house. This impossibility of staff fulfilling their care roles within working hours also serves the institutional priority on limiting expenses on resources, since staff work extra hours and must prioritize the resources they have.

# 4

# Sense-Making in the ATC

Hanging on multiple walls in the main athletic training room is a laminated piece of paper that reads:

>   NLU ATHLETIC TRAINING
>   No hats
>   No cell phones
>   No electronics
>   No headphones
>
>   Allowed in the
>   Athletic Training Room

Despite this sign, the ATC is occupied by two football athletes and an athletic trainer staring intently at their phones. One of the athletes has AirPods in his ears. While there are formal "rules" written down, they are not being followed or enforced. This is just one example of how the main athletic training room prioritizes its prize profit-making program.

Differently from this, the baseball athletic training room is strict with electronics. In an observed interaction, Tanner, a white Latino men's baseball athlete, is on the seated upper body exercise machine, pedaling with one hand and using the other hand to scroll through his phone. The athletic trainer James, yells to Tanner:

> Put your phone away. In the main athletic training room, cell phones and headphones are not allowed.

Zach, a white men's baseball athlete, shouts from across the training room, "Unless you are a football player. They just walk right in with their phones."

James responds, "There *are* signs that say no electronics... but it's not enforced." His voice trails off.

## "Muddling Through"

While the ATC seems to be a classic bureaucracy, this organization does not work so formally in maintaining total role responsibility in everyday life. Instead, people engage in what the scholar Charles Lindblom (1959) calls "muddling through," which is an approach to decision-making that involves making mistakes and correcting them.[1] In the ATC, this decision-making is based on which bodies are the most valuable, that is, those of able-bodied profit-generating sport athletes.

The issue with this is that non-profit-generating sport athletes are not seen as the priority, so they feel pushed to the side, even as their athletic resources depend on the profits the profit-generating athletes produce, and even as those profits are made on the backs of those athletes' labor. But, on the other hand, the university and its programs benefit from the other sports, too, through branding, marketing, and network benefits—the university does not undertake them as charity. So, it is understandable for these athletes to expect care for their athletic labor as well. The ways the ATC and the larger university see each athlete's body often differ from how those athletes understand their own body, its labor, and its care. When people in the ATC disagree, it's often in a contest over these meanings. When something happens outside the organizational order, it's up to the individuals

---

[1]. The term "muddling through" refers to all that is involved in settling on a common interpretation of behaviors and events.

involved to interpret a novel meaning of the communication. But the presence of the organizational expectation complicates the meanings they exchange.

Chloe, a white women's cross-country/track-and-field athlete, experienced evasion in the ATC as no staff member saw her as their responsibility. Chloe explained that she was repeatedly passed from one sports medicine staff member to another. She described this as being given the "run around" when she was asking for help with her injury. Chloe states:

> You go to [a sports medicine staff member] and you think they will be able to help you and they're like, "Oh no, why are you coming to me for this? This is [a different sports medicine staff member's] job." So, you go to [the other sports medicine staff member] and they say, "Why don't you go to [a different sports medicine staff member]." And I say, "I did go to them, but they told me to go to you." So, it's just a back-and-forth thing.

Chloe expressed her frustration at being pushed from one sports medicine staff member to another, being given indirect answers, and not receiving adequate care. Such treatment would be unusual for an athlete in a program that generated profit, as many staff members might be shifted to their care. Nevertheless, Chloe's problem ought to have been accounted for within the organizational structure and the fact that it wasn't leaves Chloe to make her own meaning that is different from what the people she interacted with would have told her but follows her perception of the organization as a whole. This example also highlights issues of informal communication channels in the ATC.

While Figure 2.2 presents the formal way the organization runs as structured by the athletic department, Figure 4.1 shows the power relations as learned through observations and interviews with sports medicine staff members and injured athletes. The top middle section includes the administrative sports medicine staff (e.g., deputy athletic director, medical director, associate athletic director, senior associate athletic director, and rehabilitation coordinator), the bottom row identifies the athletic trainers and physical therapists, and the outskirts of the figure show the peripheral staff (e.g., physical therapy residents,

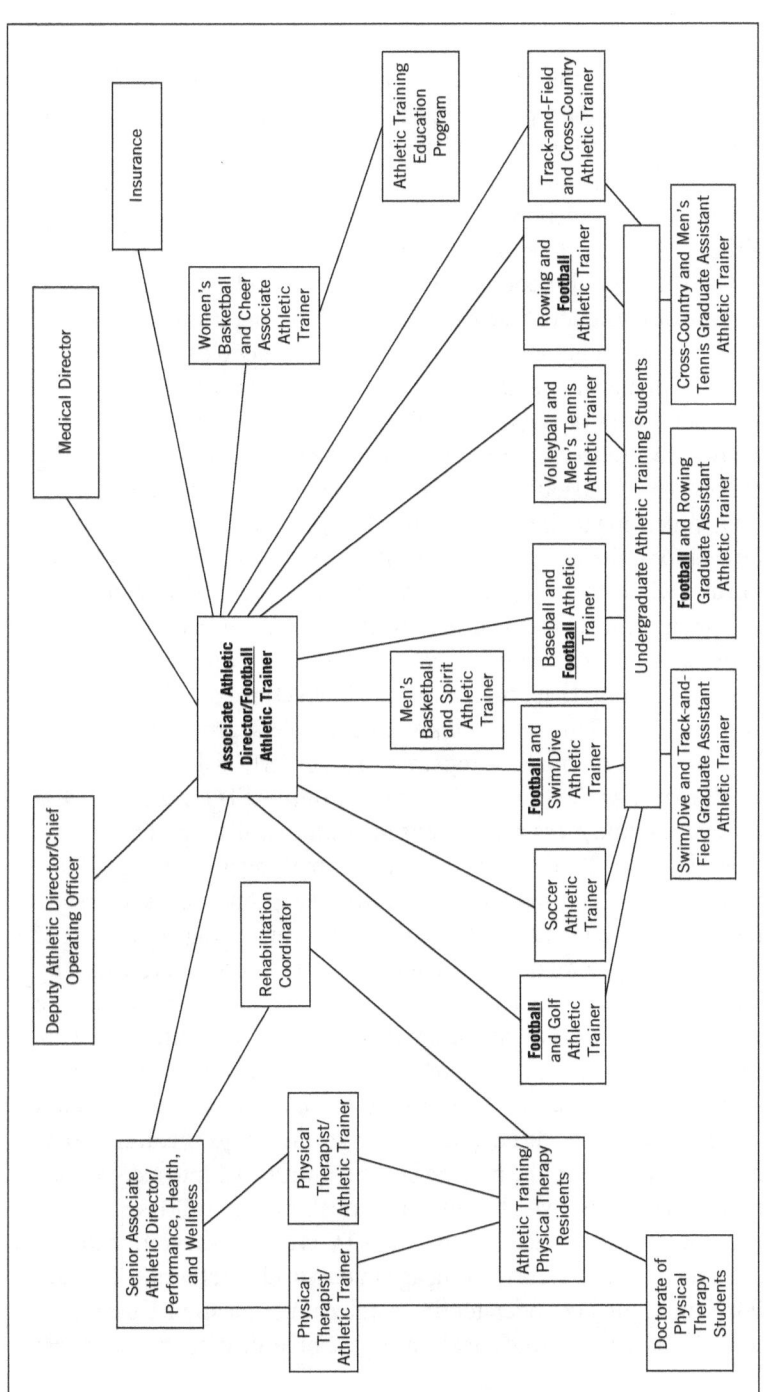

**Figure 4.1** Power relations chart of the athletic training center.

graduate physical therapy students, and undergraduate athletic training students). At the top of the figure reside the deputy athletic director and medical director who hold most of the power in the organization. The deputy athletic director aids in the day-to-day tasks and answers to the associate athletic director while the medical director is in charge of the care that athletic trainers provide.

Organizational theorist Karl Weick (2001) believes that an organization is a product of "sense-making." Differing from Lune, Weick (2001: 5) views organizations as "collections of people trying to make sense of what is happening around them"; an organization is an ongoing activity of trying to identify and coordinate interpretations of behavior. Moreover, an organization is the product of sense-making and consists of various interdependent parts, with each one contributing something to the whole. In the ATC, staff and athletes negotiate these among themselves, but the meanings that serve the organization as a whole tend to obscure how meaning is communicated.

The structure of the ATC makes ethical decision-making very difficult since the focus is on generating profit. The organization begins to make demands that obscure the real interactions people are having with one other. This sense-making, nonetheless, provides the fabric that holds an organization together in an orderly fashion.

Moreover, while the official imagery of the ATC in Figure 4.1 is bureaucratic and hierarchical, sense-making is still operating at a microlevel (Weick 2001). Specifically, sense-making is not the predominant way things are held together; rather, sense-making is the informal way interactions run. While the ATC is operating at the level of sense-making—with ongoing negotiation—this process is masked by a structural layer. The downside of this sense-making is that no one fully knows what other people are doing in the organization. The result might be what Gibson Burrell (1997) calls "organized" chaos. This is true of what is happening in the ATC. In this chaos, the athlete's body is constantly being negotiated, transformed, objectified, and commodified. Moreover, the body is being transformed into a commodity, and priority is given to the most valuable commodities.

As described in Weick (2001), the ATC is contingent and made up of sports medicine staff who engage in day-to-day activities. This activity can be further understood through communication. Communication is discussed as the backbone of the organization by the sports medicine staff. The physical therapist John uses the analogy of a sports team to understand the sports medicine staff, stating:

> Like any team, there's certain aspects and certain qualities or characteristics that's going to make that team successful. Communication has got to be huge.

Charles, a Black physician from overseas, discusses his priority for communicating with other sports medicine staff members, stating:

> There is a level of communication that is always there so that we can stay on top of what we are managing, the athlete.

Based on observations and interviews of sports medicine staff members, the staff do not use one consistent form of communication. Rather, there are different forms of communication utilized in the ATC.

The imagery of Figure 4.1 shows the official communication channels with one key administrative sports medicine staff person (i.e., the associate athletic director). While everyone is expected to follow these channels, adhering to them is difficult given the nature of the athletic training room. The important part of moving through these channels is to achieve the aims of the organization. However, findings revealed that sports medicine staff often disregard the official communication channels because they move informally through the organization for expediency.

This modus operandi is highlighted in the following example. During an interview with Elizabeth, I asked her how communication worked in the ATC. Elizabeth responds, "It is so frenetic in there and there's always a lot happening, and you get waves of people coming in," adding that most of the time if an athlete pulls a muscle at practice, effective intervention requires a quick judgment. She states, "In those circumstances, you can't really go and ask and come back." *The point is that the sports medicine staff do not have time to operate through the bureaucracy, yet they must operate within a bureaucracy.* This discrepancy highlights a major issue in bureaucratic organizations. If the main healthcare workers who care for athletes do not have time to actually participate in the organization properly, then care may be adversely affected.

Communication channels are especially difficult to follow for athletic trainers. Athletic trainers are the "first responders" in that they are the first on the scene of emergencies (i.e., injuries). As a result, athletic trainers are often unable to go through the bureaucratic channels because things need to happen immediately. Communication is also difficult for athletic trainers because they act as liaisons, conveying information between athletes and the rest of the sports medicine staff (doctors, physical therapists, psychologist, nutritionists, etc.) and reporting information about injury to coaches.

The variability in communication channels also highlights the issues associated with moving through the organization informally. There is no accountability for the actions of sports medicine staff moving informally (i.e., relaying information to athletes) because these behaviors are not recognized. What is happening in the informal organization is unofficial and thus does not have official sanctions. If a mistake is made, then everyone goes back to the structure instead of assuming accountability for actions that took place. Anything that happens in the informal organization is subject to being discredited. Moreover, in informal organizations, everything can be denied because no one is responsible (i.e., no organizational accountability). In the end, challenging an informal structure is difficult since this domain is unofficial.

In addition to the tasks mentioned earlier, athletic trainers supervise undergraduate athletic training students for their clinical hours. Undergraduate athletic training students are often in the ATC getting their clinical hours, which also acts as a time for them to learn from the athletic trainers. So, in addition to having to work in this space, the ATC is also a space to teach and learn.

Athletic trainer Derek walks over to undergraduate athletic training student Justine, and lies down on the training table in front of her. "What are we doing?" asks Derek. Without saying a word, Justine begins to examine Derek's right foot, feeling each tendon. "Okay," says Derek. Justine opens her binder to a particular page, and Derek looks at it. He pauses for a minute and takes out his phone, typing quickly. Derek then takes a pen out of his pocket and initials a page in the binder. They both walk away in separate directions. Their interaction was guided by their understandings of their roles in the organization but was otherwise quite ambiguous and little was communicated. This allows a lot of space for misunderstanding, and each party walks away making sense of the interaction based more on their general interpretation of the organizational role than on what the other person had to say.

While conducting observations at the ATC, I see instances when undergraduate athletic training students become frustrated and try to rationalize their frustration into a meaning about the normal operation of the organization as a whole. In one example, the undergraduate athletic training student Alex, a white man, is carrying medical gear back and forth to a semitruck that gets driven to away football games. "Junior year is the worst," he exclaims. Junior year is when the undergraduate athletic training students work a majority of their clinical hours. At NLU, a minimum of one hundred experience hours with a certified athletic trainer are required. These clinical hours are unpaid.

Undergraduate athletic training students are a fundamental part of the functioning of big-time college sport. Also, like the athletes, they are unpaid laborers. Noah explains:

> I was an undergraduate athletic trainer many, many years ago, and I think the biggest thing is it's an experience for these kids to learn the day-to-day operations of an athletic trainer. Obviously, I think undergraduate student athletic trainers are important to us because without them, who would help us with hydration and the little things that we need on the field. It's important, and sometimes kids don't understand that. They think, oh I'm just the water boy. No, you're not, you're a very important part of this program, but this is just what you got to do right now. I mean, I did that too. When I was a freshman [in college], I couldn't do anything but hydration. I had to make sure the water was set, the coolers were filled, and that was my job. When I was a sophomore, I got to tape, and I thought it was the greatest thing in the world. That's how it is, and here I am today.

Noah's description of the undergraduate trainees abstracts them to an ideal. In this instance, Noah is reinforcing and normalizing the unpaid labor that undergraduate athletic trainers are expected to engage in. One wonders how his sense of their work differs from theirs, but such open communication is uncommon, leaving space for meaning-making.

Athletic trainers have significant responsibility in this organization. Given their busy schedules, athletic trainers were observed explaining an exercise to an injured athlete and then leaving the athlete to perform the exercise alone. Since athletic trainers are so busy with other tasks, they did not always have the time to give athletes their full attention and watch to ensure that they are performing their exercises correctly.

Given the way the ATC actually operates daily, this organization is better understood as "loosely coupled" (Bittner 1990; Silverman 1971; Weick 2001). With this terminology, Weick (2001) is attempting to move away from structural imagery and trying to reveal how people make sense of the ambiguous day-to-day interactions they have with others in the organization. On the other hand, if the ATC organization were structural, the interactions would be clear. However, this structural organization is not the reality in the ATC. Implied by this notion of loosely coupled is that people are interpreting what they are doing and attempting to convince others that the positions they are taking on are valid. The interactions that are occurring within the organization are not clear-cut and, therefore, must be reconciled on an ongoing basis. This process is never settled; there may be momentary clarity, but obscurity is ongoing.

There is a social imagery associated with the bureaucratic framework. This imagery serves to reinforce the organization. Within this imagery, there is an associated chain of command. However, in everyday life, people realize that things must get done in ways that often go around this chain of command because the bureaucracy does not always operate effectively.

Instead of abiding by the hierarchy of the organization, sports medicine staff members move in a way that is outside of this structure. In reality, the sports medicine staff are just trying to fill organizational demands but do not understand that sense-making is happening, specifically how their roles are being negotiated. For example, during an interview with Anne, a white Latina athletic trainer and physical therapist, I asked her if there were any parts of the job that were not in the job description. Anne explained that every day in the ATC is different. Therefore, there is a multitude of daily tasks that need to be completed that are referred to as "duties as assigned." In order words, every day different tasks need to be completed, and most times those tasks are not known until they must be performed. While attempting to make sense of the organization, on a day-to-day basis there are many interactions in which decisions are constantly debated and questioned, thereby transforming the ATC into a contested terrain: a space where meanings are not clear and participants can make claims to different interpretations.

## Contested Terrain within a Bureaucratic Organization

An organization that has sense-making operating at its core is a contested terrain. Within this bureaucratic framework, which serves to stabilize the organization, everyday tasks still need to be completed. According to R. Edwards (1979), contested terrains have come into existence due to hierarchical workplaces that are ruled from the top down but are dysfunctional in carrying out their everyday practices. One reason the ATC is a contested terrain results from the intersection of the formal and informal aspects of this formal organization. In other words, the ATC is a contested terrain because the organization presents itself as formal while functioning as an informal structure.

This conflict may explain why there is a shift to having specialized skill sets in the ATC—for example, sport psychologist, nutritionist—to make this contested terrain less problematic. Introducing these skills makes the bureaucracy more refined so that, at least in theory, contentiousness would be reduced as different specialists take domain over different questions. In this way, a degree of variability is built into the organization by design. But this maneuver may only delay conflict, possibly making the bureaucracy less flexible and responsive to the full range of questions that slip through the cracks, thereby forcing people again to make decisions in sense-making mode.

Organizations operate within a field; when actors enter this field, according to the sociologist Pierre Bourdieu ([1984] 2012), they enter with their agenda based on their social locations. The ATC is the epicenter of all of those institutional actors who have agendas and perspectives that are negotiated with others. Within this space, for example, everyone has different conceptions or definitions of injury.

Due to these differences, the definition of injury is constantly negotiated. Therefore, this space is a contested terrain, particularly in terms of how the medical staff provides treatments to athletes (i.e., techniques of athletic training). The athletic training room, specifically the main athletic training room, is a contested terrain when understood in terms of the different stocks of knowledge operating within this component of the sport institution (R. Edwards 1979; Toombs 1992). For example, the definition of injury is negotiated based on the organization of the athletic training room. This practice depends on the sports that are prioritized as well as the techniques used for treatments. The athletic training room is the epicenter of all this activity.

## Conclusions

The organizational issues discussed in this chapter mediate and inform the care that should be provided to injured athletes (which is the stated purpose of the ATC). The constraints on staffing available in a given moment, a cultural ambiguity of interaction and norms, and the overbearing company line serve to obscure the day-to-day interactions. In the absence of clarity in small interactions and the dominance of organizational roles and orientation, different participants walk away with their own meanings that differ from those of others around them. These findings call for reflection on the appropriateness of the bureaucratic structure. The shortcomings discussed are not due to a lack of desire to aid athletes but rather result from the structure of the organization and the accompanying exploitation and objectification of bodies. In other words, rather than these problems being linked to the individual choices of the sports medicine staff, they occur because of the structure of the organization itself, which uses bureaucracy, in-house care, and understaffing to protect the organizational priorities and leaves the day-to-day interactions to the whims of individual meaning-making. Since these staff members have been imbued with the stock of knowledge and prevailing rules of the organization, it should not be surprising that the organizational orientation and prevailing social norms influence their treatment of athletes. The structure of this organization has also re-created power structures in the athletic training room that sports medicine staff are trying to fight.

Athlete healthcare operates within organizational constraints. As discussed in this chapter, the organization of this institutionalized healthcare influences the care provided. The ATC must act informally but formal structure conceals a lot of the conflict that is occurring. Moreover, in this informal space, sense-making is in operation. When sense-making is in effect in the contested terrain of the ATC, the objectification of athletes can sometimes be somewhat concealed—even if the organization understands it is exploiting an athlete for profit or an athletic training student on staff, others in the same space may come to a different conclusion about the aims of the organization. According to interviews with sports medicine staff, the well-being and safety of athletes is the most important aspect of the job. While sports medicine staff believe that athlete well-being is at the forefront of their work, that meaning is neutralized by the organizational orientation toward profit. Staff work for NLU and the NLU athletic department and act within the goals of the NCAA. Dialogue is said to be at the heart of the patient-centeredness espoused by the NCAA (Courson et al. 2014; NCAA 2019b). However, sports medicine staff do not always have time to be patient-centered and engage the athletes regularly in dialogue. The next chapters extend these findings and examine data from gendered and racialized standpoints.

# 5

## The Gendered Nature of Healthcare in Big-Time College Sport

In the main athletic training room, television stations, such as ESPN, ESPNEWS, and ESPNU, that focus on profit-generating men's sports (i.e., football, basketball, and baseball) are always playing on the television. When I first start my observations, a sports medicine staff member, John, asks me what I am looking for. I responded that I am looking for patterns. John asks if I have seen anything yet. I say that one pattern I notice is that men's sports, specifically football, are often played on the televisions in the ATC. John responds:

> Have you ever seen the show *Different Strokes*? It is a famous show from the 70s that was really good, and people left the reruns on to watch. That is what is happening with the televisions here. They are just on, and no one changes it, it just is.

While unintentional, this response is illustrative of the dominant gender ideology of masculinity in the ATC. Men's sports and masculinity is seen as the norm. It just is. The sport scholar Cheryl Cooky and colleagues Michael Messner, and Michela Musto (2015) discuss this idea that men's sports are almost always covered in sports media while women's sports receive less attention, even though there is a dramatic increase in women's sports participation since the passing of Title IX.

## Post (?) Title IX

Title IX of the Education Amendment Act of 1972 was originally implemented to deal with sex discrimination faced by women in higher education in the United States (Ware 2007). According to the U.S. Department of Education (2021):

> No person in the United States shall, on the basis of sex, be excluded from participation in, be denied the benefits of, or be subjected to discrimination under any education program or activity receiving federal financial assistance.

Since implementation of this legislation, there has been more prominence brought to women's collegiate sport in the United States. In one important application, Title IX aids in gender equity in sport by prohibiting the exclusion of women from participating in or benefiting from educational programs or activities that receive federal financial assistance (U.S. Department of Education 2021).

While there has been progress with the passing of Title IX over fifty years ago, there is still gender discrimination and sexism that affects the healthcare athletes receive in the ATC. In this gendered ideology, women are seen as physically inferior to men and given a secondary status (Twin 1979). Within gender, there is hegemonic masculinity, which is the dominant or most idealized form of masculinity that can be reflected in embodied practices (Connell 1987). Throughout sport, the domination of men is thus made to appear only logical. This has implications for women athletes. During an interview, I ask Chloe if she felt that her sport received the same kind of treatment from sports medicine staff members as other sports. She responded:

> I think for the most part everyone's equal. Football, I think, gets more attention just because there's so many of them and they are actually going through a car accident every day at practice, basically with their hits and whatever. So, I think it's fair. I don't know.

Chloe is discussing how football is prioritized and then goes on to justify this by the physical aspect of the sport, comparing it to getting hit by a car. She then backtracks and second guesses what she has said.

While all sports were compared to football in the main athletic training room, women's rowing was uniquely discriminated against. Women's rowing had the second largest roster next to football (65 athletes vs. 117 athletes, respectively), and, in interviews with athletes, rowing was often described as the "Title IX sport" that was used to balance out larger men's sports teams such as football. Whether this is true or not, calling rowing a "Title IX sport" is very telling. And, even though rowing has a roster size comparable to football, this team is not given the same access to or care from the sports medicine staff. For example, the football team has six sports medicine staff members that look after the team, one of whom works only with football, while rowing has two sports medicine staff members who split their time with football. This allocation is illustrative of gendered organizational inequity. In this case, the organization of the ATC is contributing to health inequities that result from systems of oppression and structural factors that cause disproportionate harm and frustrate Title IX's promise of equal access to healthcare.

Lily, a white international women's rowing athlete, discusses her distaste of being treated differently than football players. She states:

> I put my body through just as much shit as every single other person in this training room. . . . I've waited my time, I've warmed up on the XF5, I've foam rolled, I've done all the stuff. Why am I being pushed back? Then I thought, "[Lily], don't be stupid. This is a Title IX sport."

In this instance, Lily shows how she internalized the sexism and gender discrimination she has experienced in the ATC and justifies that she is being treated differently in this space because she plays what is deemed a "Title IX sport," women's rowing. This is due to the idea that has been pushed onto her since she arrived at NLU: rowing is a Title IX sport that is around only to even out large football teams. While it has been over forty-seven years (1976) since Chris Ernst and fellow Yale rowers protested for equality post the enactment of Title IX, we are still seeing gender inequality at play.

## The Social Construction of Gender

The patriarchal ideals that were brought with the colonization of the United States have resulted in the stereotyping of the dominant gender expression of masculinity. The philosopher Simone de Beauvoir (1949), who was influenced greatly by the philosopher Jean-Paul Sartre (1948), argued that both sex and gender are socially constructed. According to de Beauvoir (1949), women (and men) are not born, they are made. Gender is a social construction (Berger and Luckmann 1966).[1] However, the duality of masculinity and femininity is seen as real to those in the ATC and affects how athletes and sports medicine staff make sense of injury and move through this space. The scholars Candace West and Don Zimmerman (1987) argue that gender is both a routine that women and men engage in and are guided by the social norms of masculinity and femininity. This social construction of gender is reified in organizations, particularly in the ATC.

Terrence, a white men's football athlete who recently experienced a knee injury, is receiving STIM in the main athletic training room. STIM is a treatment that uses electrical stimulation to treat muscle spasms and pain. Terrence winces at each electrical pulse that surges through his body. An athletic trainer, Oliver, is watching Terrence get treatment from across the main athletic training room. Oliver shouts over to Terrence, "Take it like a stripper!" "What . . ." says Terrence, his eyebrows are furrowed with a shocked and confused look on his face. Oliver's comment is inferring that he expects Terrence to act tough and not show that he is in pain. This is a result of the dominant ideology of masculinity. Within this gendered ideology, men are expected to express themselves in a masculine manner (e.g., tough, machismo) and to respect the typical masculine role (i.e., profit-generating sport athletes). This then becomes the norm, instead of accepting that pain can be experienced by men. So, the dominant ideology of masculinity that men should not express pain is enforced. Oliver even goes a step further to sexualize the pain Terrence is experiencing. He tells Terrence to "take it like a stripper," as if to insinuate that in sex work

---

1. The sociologists Peter Berger and Thomas Luckmann (1966) conceived the theory of the social construction of reality, which is the process in which people continuously create, through their actions and interactions, a shared reality.

pain is normal. As Oliver believes sex work does, so, too, does he normalize the commercialization of the body's pain in athletic work. This is what the sociologist of sport and health Don Sabo (2009: 146) calls the "pain principle," which he defines as "a patriarchal cultural belief that pain is inevitable, and that the endurance of pain enhances one's cultural and moral worth." Sabo argues that definitions of pain, and sport injury, are gendered. For example, since sport is often equated to masculinity, denying pain in sport is masculine.

## Masculinity in the ATC

This gendered ideology was also found to occur in the baseball athletic training room, a predominantly male space. The philosopher Judith Butler (1988) argues that all people engage in gender "performance" to survive, which is the case for athletes who perform the gendered ideology of masculinity. As she states, "Discrete genders are part of what 'humanizes' individuals in contemporary culture; indeed, those who fail to do their gender right are regularly punished" (Butler 1988: 522). Similarly, the scholar Ann Hall (1985) argues that sport is a male-dominated institution and a cultural practice that sustains domination and subordination. In sport, particularly in the ATC, the dominant gender ideology of masculinity is reproduced.

Loud music is always playing in the baseball athletic training room, and today the infamous Bubba Sparxxx's "Ms. New Booty" rings throughout the room. The baseball training room is roughly a quarter of the size of the main athletic training room, with three athletic training tables (as opposed to the twenty-six in the main athletic training room). Athletes are receiving treatment on the training tables when one of the coaches, a man, walks in boisterously laughing. He goes up to each athlete in the room, punching them hard in the shoulder. Josh, a white men's baseball athlete, who is sitting on one of the athletic training tables getting treatment for his recent shoulder surgery watches with caution. When the coach gets to Josh, he turns his face and winces as if to prepare himself for the punch while telling the coach he can't move this arm (pointing to his shoulder). The coach pauses for a moment, as if to rethink, then punches Josh in the uninjured shoulder.

While profit-generating sport athletes are prioritized in the ATC, there is still a gendered atmosphere that affects all athletes. The sociologist Michael Messner (1992) argues that sport plays a role in the creation and maintenance of notions of masculinity. The need to perform the ideal male gender was commonly pushed onto men athletes by men sports medicine staff members, as shown by Josh being forced to be masculine even though he recently underwent surgery and is in the process of rehabilitating.

Some men athletes attempt to accept these gender ideologies because it increases their social status, thereby allowing them to receive better care. Other athletes are abiding by the "sport ethic," which the sociologists Robert Hughes and Jay Coakley (1991) describe as an overconformity to the norms and values of sport. These norms and values include making sacrifices for the game, striving for distinction, accepting risks, playing through pain, and refusing to accept limits. Athletes feel pressure to maintain a high level of athletic performance, and, at times, they have to respond to major events such as injuries. For example, Jack discusses what he would do when he would experience injury. He states:

> I'd block someone or hit someone, and then I couldn't feel my arm. But I'm thinking, tough it out, football. I'm thinking this is part of it.

Jack was on track to be a top draft pick in the NFL. This notion of toughing it out follows sociologist Robert Turner's (2018) concept of "football habitus," where football athletes internalize the norms of a progression to the professional league. Injury is a part of this norm. Similarly, Kalman-Lamb (2018) argues that a culture of masculinity is created in the sport system that expects players to play through pain, and, in this setting, players are aware that they are doing so in the interest of others.

However, athletes have different understandings of "toughness." To some, there is physical toughness and there is mental toughness. Ray, a Black men's cross-country/track-and-field athlete explains, "I think football is pretty mentally tough too, but it's not as mentally tough as track to me."

## The ATC as a Gendered Organization

Organizations are a place where widely disseminated cultural images of gender are invented and reproduced (Acker 1990; Hearn and Parkin 1987). According to Acker (1990: 146), for an organization to be gendered, "advantage and disadvantage, exploitation and control, action and emotion, meaning and identity, are patterned through and in terms of a distinction between male and female, masculine and feminine."

In the ATC, there is a clear distinction between masculine and feminine. All athletes are exposed to the male gaze, or in the main athletic training room: the football gaze.[2] That is, athletes are looked at using a masculine sport lens in the ATC. Based on this practice, the dominant gender ideology in the ATC is that of masculinity in sport. This dominant gender ideology of masculinity affects both women and men since both nontraditional men's sports (i.e., tennis, diving, cross-country, track) and women's sports are peripheral to traditional masculine sports (i.e., football, baseball, basketball) in the ATC. Since profit-generating sport athletes are viewed as the most masculine, this bias has consequences for non-profit-generating sport athletes, including men. For example, during an interview with Sam, a white international men's tennis athlete, he explains that the bodies of other sports athletes are often compared to the bodies of football athletes, because football athletes are seen as strong and experience the most brutal injuries. Sam states:

> If you look at injuries in football, and then tennis and track, they're going to be wildly different because, in football, you can play through a fracture to some degree, or whatever. Because those guys, they're tough, and they do what they have to do because they're told to do what they have to do. But then, you look at a sport like track, and you're talking about milliseconds. And if someone has a tweak in their calf, not even an injury, a soreness. That could affect them by point whatever milliseconds,

---

2. This differentiation can further be understood through Sartre (1956), who discussed the concept of the gaze, which was further built on by Mulvey (1975), who discussed the male gaze.

and that's mentally frustrating. And then coaches and administrators look at the difference, and there's this football guy playing through a broken leg, and you have a muscle soreness. "What are you a little girl?" That's what they literally say.

Since the view that football athletes are tough dominates in the ATC, other sports are constantly compared to football. This judgment is also an example of relative masculinity since, in this case, football is seen as hegemonic, or, in sports discourse, as the "most" masculine. In the ATC, sports medicine staff and athletes reinforce hegemonic masculinity by constructing football as the reference point of masculinity based on bodily injury and pain (Gramsci 1995). Furthermore, stereotyping non-profit-generating men athletes and women athletes as weak reinforces masculinity, in general, for profit-generating sport athletes and their bodies.

The ATC is centered around football, a profit-generating sport that is viewed as masculine. Due to this, athletes' injuries are often compared to those that football athletes experience. Differing from profit-generating sport athletes such as football players, non-profit-generating sport athletes do not receive the same level of attention and care. This appears to be due to both a perception that the injuries of non-profit-generating sport athletes are not as serious compared to the injuries of profit-generating sport athletes and the emphasis put on profit-generating sport athletes being masculine. Moreover, non-profit-generating sport athletes are not seen as valuable a commodity as profit-generating sport athletes.

## Consequences of Constructions of Gender on Sports Medicine Staff Members

The dominant ideology of gender, particularly hegemonic masculinity, is also reflected among sports medicine staff members. For example, all of the leadership positions (i.e., administrative sports medicine staff) in the ATC are held by men, which serves to reinforce this ideology. In addition to this, the dominant gender ideology is pushed onto sports medicine staff members, which can be seen in the following observed interaction.

Elizabeth is standing in a circle with two other DPT residents Rick—a white man—and Lindsay—a white woman. Elizabeth is attempting to come up with questions to quiz them on. The physical therapist John walks over, and Elizabeth tells him she is trying to think of questions with which to quiz them. John takes over and begins quizzing them. He gives an example about women's soccer and an agility test he gave them. He explains how the team was timed running forward, shuffling to the right, shuffling to the left, and then backpedaling. He asks, given that a majority of the women's soccer team kicks with their right feet, what direction do they believe would be the strongest direction for them? Elizabeth and Lindsay engage in a conversation to try and figure it out. Lindsay gets out of her seat and begins reenacting the movements, shuffling to the right then the left, then a short sprint, then a backpedal. By process of elimination, they decide the strongest movement for a right-footed soccer player is between the right and left shuffle. John then asks about mobility techniques. Lindsay talks about the jumping jack circuit. John tells Lindsay to run through the circuit with Rick as the patient. Lindsay then runs Rick through the circuit. First, regular jumping jacks. Next, the feet doing the movement of regular jumping jacks (out and in), but the arms are moving forward and backward. Rick is having a hard time doing the movement. He keeps stopping and laughing saying he can't do it. "Man up," says John in a stern tone. Rick looks taken aback and responds, "Why don't the rest of them [Elizabeth and Lindsay] have to do it?" John says because he is the professor, Elizabeth has her DPT, and Lindsay is the one asking the questions. John is being significantly tougher on Rick. While still going through the circuit, with each wrong move or word John tells Rick "come on, man." After roughly an hour of "quizzing," John says, "that is all I have for the day" and walks away. Since notions of gender are pushed onto sports medicine staff members and then embodied, this, in turn, affects how these individuals treat athletes.

## Conclusions

In the main athletic training room, there is a mural of former athletes from each sport that the university has (women's and men's cross-country, women's swimming and diving, men's diving, women's and men's tennis, women's and men's track-and-field, women's golf, women's rowing, women's soccer, and women's volleyball). While this makes it seem as though each athlete is equal in this space, thus receiving the same care, this is a facade. This mural is performative and not representative of who is being privileged in this space. Those who are privileged are profit-generating sport athletes. However, this gendered nature of the ATC affects *all* athletes. *Sport, specifically the ATC, is a site where gender meanings are constructed in specific ways.* Masculinity and being a man are seen as dominant; therefore, those who do not subscribe to that are treated differently or as less than. These gender differences in organizations are due to their structure and not to the characteristics of the individual (Kanter 1977). The purpose of this is for the organization to keep order or maintain power so that the ATC can generate profit.

# 6

# The Racialized Nature of Healthcare in Big-Time College Sport

Jared, Luke, and Darien, all Black men's football athletes, are sitting quietly next to each other on athletic training tables while on their phones. The athletic trainer Brian, a white man, comes out of his office and exclaims, "[Luke] is like a dog who doesn't realize that [his owner] is gone but he waits around looking for him." The athletic trainer Oliver, another white man, laughs at this comment and follows by stating that Brian is an "outstanding citizen," reinforcing this dominant ideology of the servile relationship between athlete and institution. Jared is visibly upset and stands up for his teammate, responding to Oliver, "The fuck?" Darien, whispers to Jared to be respectful. Jared protests, "I don't disrespect someone unless I feel disrespected by them." A few minutes later, Jared walks over to Oliver from behind and grabs his shoulders tightly and whispers in his ear, "Imma fuck you up." Oliver smiles nervously and pushes Jared away forcefully. Luke says to Jared, "I read what you said on your lips." "What did I say?" Jared asks. "You said you're gonna fuck him up," responds Luke. "Yeah," says Jared smiling.

In this interaction, Brian dehumanizes Luke when referring to him as an animal. Jared does not appreciate this stereotype and challenges Brian, which results in another athlete, who appears to go along with this dominant ideology that views the white men sports medicine staff as superior, attempting to stop Jared. After all, there is a sort of value exchanged in the transaction between the athlete and the institution, and it would be disappointing to lose the benefit. The higher education scholar Siduri Haslerig along with colleagues Rican Vue, and Sara Grummert (2020) discuss that the consequences of dehumanization include the desensitization to the pain and injury by others. This example of a sports medicine staff member using a stereotype in referring to a Black athlete reinforces the notion that Black men athletes are inferior to the white men sports medicine staff and desensitizes their pain in the eyes of those who would, according to the NCAA's mission, be their caregivers. According to Victor Ray (2019), this is a racialized process in which white sports medicine staff are elevating their group by subordinating another, the Black athletes. In this racialized space, the dominant ideology of whiteness is reinforced through the mechanism of stereotyping (Steele and Aronson 1995; Steele 1997).

## Whiteness in the ATC

As a PWI, NLU and its ATC are founded on white supremacy, which allows for white privilege. White supremacy is the background for understanding the social construction of race in ATCs. Race has been socially constructed to establish power for whites and oppression of nonwhites (Lopez 1996). A consequence of white supremacy and the social construction of race is racism. Racism is defined as any prejudice against people because of their race when those views are reinforced by systems of power (Oluo 2018). The sociologist Herbert Blumer (1958) argues that racism is a reaction to any threat that would disrupt the racial hierarchy.

Moreover, PWIs have white supremacist and anti-Blackness foundations. In these spaces, Blackness is often presented in opposition to whiteness. The sport scholar Ajhanai Keaton (2022) argues that college sport is a site of cultural reproduction where actors make sense of whiteness and anti-Blackness. Keaton (2021) also argues that whiteness is reified in institutions through abstract liberalism, whiteness as property, and color blindness.

Whiteness is a socially constructed ideology that can result in those who are perceived as not fitting in (people of color) being pushed to the periphery. However, because whiteness is constructed as universal, this designation is easily missed. Whiteness is a credential. This condition means that being white, as opposed to nonwhite, allows access to organizational resources (Ray 2019: 16). Moreover, whiteness is used for access to healthcare in the ATC.

Whiteness is prevalent in the NCAA and HEIs (Hextrum 2021; Hextrum and Sethi 2021). The sport scholars Joshua Vadeboncoeur and Trevor Bopp (2020) apply sociologist Elijah Anderson's (2015) concept to argue that college sport is a "white space" where Black athletes are marginalized into certain sports and unseen in administrative or coaching positions. They further argue that whiteness upholds structural racism in college sport.

In the case of the ATC studied, all administrative sports medicine staff are white (white non-Latinx and white Latinx). In this regard, whiteness is the reference point in the ATC. *The point is that sports medicine staff seem to accept the ideology of whiteness because this behavior increases their social status.*

This follows the sociologist Douglas Hartmann (2001: 405) who argues that sport is a contested racial terrain where "racial images, ideologies, and inequalities are constructed, transformed, and constantly struggled over." He goes on to say that to understand sport as a contested racial terrain, we must also understand the racial order in the United States. This racial order has been put in place through settler colonialism and racial capitalism and is exacerbated by neoliberalism. Within the contested racial terrain of the ATC, all those in power are white, which affects the meanings of race. This has created a dichotomy between Black and white athletes. Specifically, Black athletes are often discussed in terms of their athleticism (Carrington 2010) and are often portrayed as physically violent and anti-intellectual (Shropshire and Williams 2017), while white athletes are discussed in terms of their intellectual abilities. H. Edwards (1984) argues that the "dumb jock" narrative that has been put onto Black athletes is not natural but rather has been constructed by society; however, this construction has real consequences.

It is 6:50 A.M., and football athletes have been filing in and out of the main athletic training room for the past hour. The athletic trainer Nancy is taping a line of football athletes before practice. As one athlete hops off the athletic training table, Miles, a Black men's football athlete, walks toward the table for his turn. "How are you this morning?" asks Nancy. Miles does not respond. Nancy looks at Miles with disdain and repeats loud and slow, "HOW... ARE... YOU... THIS... MORNING?" "Good," responds Miles quietly, in a taken aback tone. "Alright," says Nancy sarcastically as she quickly tapes Miles's wrist. She shouts, "Next!" with her eyebrows raised, looking at the athlete waiting in line. This interaction not only reinforces her authority in the eyes of the system they share but poses Miles as not smart enough to understand her words in normal speech, as if there could be no other reason for an athlete not to answer her.

## The ATC as a Racialized Organization

Race is ever apparent in the ATC organization. The sociologist Victor Ray (2019) argues that organizations are racial structures. According to Ray (2019: 11), racialized organizations are "meso-level social structures that limit the personal agency and collective efficacy of subordinate racial groups while magnifying the agency of the dominant racial group."

Ray develops four tenets to highlight racialized organizations. First, racialized organizations enhance or diminish the agency of racial groups. Second, racialized organizations legitimate the unequal distribution of resources. Third, whiteness is a credential. And fourth, the decoupling of formal rules from organizational practice is often racialized.

In October 2020, Victor Ray appeared on *The End of Sport Podcast* with hosts and sport scholars Derek Silva, Johanna Mellis, and Nathan Kalman-Lamb. In this episode, he discusses his article "A Theory of Racialized Organizations" (Ray 2019) and argues that racism is not in but rather *of* sport organizations. Keaton and sport scholar Joseph Cooper (2022) argue that the NCAA is a racialized organization where racial marginalization is maintained and sustained.

The sport scholars Joseph Cooper, Akuoma Nwadike, and Charles Macaulay (2017) utilize CRT to investigate how five NCAA "race neutral" policies contribute to racialized outcomes. The findings from this study reveal that the NCAA lags behind other sport organizations for diversity. Cooper and colleagues suggest that a culturally responsive program be provided (cultural competence).

Race plays a central role in the organization of contemporary society. The sociologist W.E.B. Du Bois ([1903] 1989) believed that a major issue in modern times is the color line, or racial segregation. According to the sociologist Joe Feagin (2006: 2), the United States is the "only major Western country founded on racial oppression." Moreover, the sociologist Eduardo Bonilla-Silva (2001) believes that many struggles in society, or a racialized social system, contain a racial component. In *Faces at the Bottom of the Well*, Derrick Bell (1993) discusses how racism is an integral part of U.S. society. According to Feagin (2006), racism is systemic and is built into, or embedded in, the routine operation of American institutions. Using this logic, racism is embedded in the university setting, the American healthcare system, and the institution of sport. Racism is both ideological and operational because this practice is built into the ideologies and institutions of society, negatively affecting people of color.

While the Civil Rights Act of 1964 prohibits discrimination based on race in public places and federally funded programs, still, race discrimination occurs. Even the sociologists James Frey and Stanley Eitzen (1991) argue that race discrimination occurs in sport.

In the ATC, race is intrinsically intertwined into the organization. One way we can see this is in the use of racialized language, such as the term "oversee." According to the NCAA (2024c):

> The employees at the NCAA's national office *oversee* all championships, manage programs that benefit student-athletes and support member committees that make rules and policies for college sports.

In conversations with sports medicine staff members, the term "oversee" was often used. In an interview with Noah, I ask him what his job is, and he responds, "I *oversee* the whole athletic training department." Similarly, athletic trainer Brian, a white man, discusses an athlete's rehabilitation process, stating:

> I *oversee* what's going on, know how their progression is, know when is the next time they have to follow up with doc, and everything like that.

In the plantation system the term "overseer" was used to refer to the person who directed the daily work of slaves. This same racialized language is used today in the ATC.

## Racialization of Pain

In addition to the university, healthcare system, and sport being racialized, so is pain in the ATC. This racialization of pain sees skin color and experiencing pain differently. This results in Black men not being believed about the pain they are experiencing (Washington 2006).

It is 6:10 A.M. in the main athletic training room, and Maria is talking to Tyson, a Black men's track-and-field athlete. Tyson tells Maria he will not be able to make it through practice because of the pain he has in his right quad. Maria looks perplexed and tells Tyson to lie on the training table on his back with his legs up in the air at a ninety-degree angle. Maria pushes Tyson's right leg toward his head and then back. She asks if he feels a sharp pain or if it feels tight. He responds, "sharp pain." Maria then has Tyson sit on the edge of the table with his right leg straight and raise it up and down. "Higher," says Maria each time Tyson lifts his leg. Maria then tells Tyson to bend his knee toward his chest then straighten it. He does not seem to be able to draw his leg back toward his chest as Maria is asking, so she grabs his foot and pushes it back forcefully. Tyson groans loudly. The athlete's eyes are closed, and his teeth are clenched together; he looks like he is in pain. Maria tells Tyson "Your hips are incredibly tight, not in pain. Do you foam roll?" Tyson says yes. Maria responds, "Do you really do it or do you guys' kind of half ass it?" He said he does it, she says okay, looking as though she believes him. Tyson is lying on his back again, Maria is coaching him to breathe in and out, and she pushes his leg forward and backward (his leg is at a ninety-degree angle). Maria tells the athlete to do an A skip march as she watches intently, correcting his form with each step. She then asks him to do a B skip. The athlete begins, and Maria's face looks confused. She corrects him, telling him to lead with his heel. He does it wrong again. Maria asks him if he knows how to do a B skip. He says, "Yeah, it's just hard to walk." "No, it isn't," responds Maria. She asks him how it feels. "Uhhh . . ." he responds. She says she wants to make sure he can do a body weight squat before he is sent back out to practice. She asks him if it feels like a tightness or a pull. "A little bit of a pull," he says. "Let me go consult with [my superior]," says Maria. After a few minutes, Maria walks back, and Tyson leaps off the table he has been sitting on and exclaims, "Ow!" This is Tyson's final attempt to overemphasize his pain to Maria and his inability to engage certain physical activities. He asks if he is going back to practice. Maria responds, "What is the point of pulling a quad when all we need are bodies to cross the finish line." Tyson's entire body relaxes as he drops his head back with a sigh of relief.

Throughout this interaction, Tyson's notions of pain are being deflected and denied by Maria. Tyson attempts to exaggerate his pain to Maria, and it is not until after a forty-five-minute evaluation that she believes his pain (or gives up fighting him on it) and allows him to sit out of practice. In closing, she underlines the objective of her work as sending an adequate number of bodies across the finish line.

## Conclusions

Big-time college sport is exploitative in a racialized way. *A key point is that since the meaning of race is constructed and dominant ideologies of whiteness are enforced in the ATC, the meaning of health and injury is also constructed, in a manner that creates health inequities between profit-generating and non-profit-generating sport athletes.* Power must also be recognized to properly understand the social relations that exist.

# 7

# Intersectional Experiences in College Athlete Healthcare

While Title IX seemingly benefits all women athletes, it has been most beneficial to white women athletes, while still marginalizing women athletes of color who sit at this intersection. Intersectionality, a term coined by the scholar Kimberlé Crenshaw (1989), highlights that people are often affected not only by their race but also by their gender, sexual orientation, class, age, and global location. The proposition of intersectionality is a way of thinking about the compounding social locations that, for example, women of color experience that allow us to understand how issues are not just a race problem nor just a gender problem but rather a race and a gender problem. By studying the convergence of race stereotypes and gender stereotypes, the health inequities that exist at the nexus of gender and race can be better understood.

The sociologist Felecia Theune (2019) argues that Title IX does not provide the same opportunities to Black women athletes as white women athletes. Similarly, the sport scholars Courtney Flowers, Jasmine Hamilton, and Joyce Olushola Ogunrinde (2023) argue that Title IX is a "single axis" equity law that is harmful to Black women in college sport due to their intersectional identity. Moreover, the scholars Tomika Ferguson and James Satterfield (2016) argue that Black women athletes contradict norms of femininity, which are synonymous with white women, therefore, these women utilize hyper femininity to cope with their "outsider within" status in the world. Similarly, Hextrum (2021) argues that there is an expectation for women athletes to act feminine that is often tied to whiteness.

Non-profit-generating women of color athletes are at an extreme disadvantage because they do not benefit the university financially, nor do they adhere to the dominant ideologies of masculinity or whiteness. The sport scholars Akilah R. Carter-Francique and Courtney L. Flowers (2013) show in their work how dominant ideologies play a role in the sporting lives of women of color resulting them in being seen as "other."

The problem of prioritization of care for profit-generating sport athletes and dominant ideologies of masculinity and whiteness is exacerbated for women of color in non-profit-generating sports, given the compounding dominant gender and race ideologies. The utilization of one of the propositions of CRT, intersectionality (Crenshaw 1989), allows us to further understand how the ATC operates in a discriminatory and unequal manner that perpetuates the marginalization of athletes by race and gender.

Moreover, utilizing the concept of intersectionality facilitates our understanding of how power relates to the issues of access and success. Women of color face discrimination not only by race but also by gender. The intersection of these various social considerations may affect the care that athletes receive. In this regard, intersectionality is a way of thinking about identity and power in relationships. The political scientist Evelyn Simien and colleagues Nneka Arinze and Jennifer McGarry (2019) argue for the utilization of Black feminist theories, including intersectionality, because it enables Black women athletes to have a voice and become more visible, which is often not the case in the literature on this population.

Keeping intersectionality in mind, the sociologist Crystal Fleming (2018) argues that white male supremacy socializes people to devalue the critical insights of Black women and girls. The findings of the current study are consistent with this position. For example, Mary, an Asian women's swimming and diving athlete and international student, in discussing her back injury, compares it to a fellow white man athlete. Mary states, "[My injury] is not as bad as [Ben—a teammate who is a white man]." However, she continues to discuss how her injury causes her to have "excruciating pain." She continues by saying, "I don't cry, and I cried."

For women of color, the dominant ideologies of gender and race are reinforced through the mechanism of evasion. Evasion is conceptualized as an attempt to avoid a situation by giving excuses. The sociologist Tressie McMillan Cottom (2019) discusses in her book *Thick* how mechanisms of evasion are common among healthcare professionals who attempt to deny Black women competence over their own body. This mechanism of evasion and denying Black women competence over their body was apparent in this study and is highlighted in the following example.

Taylor, a Black women's track-and-field athlete, complains of pain in her wrist. At first, the sports medicine staff told Taylor that she was probably experiencing pain because she has extra bones in her wrist. To help her with the pain, she was put into a splint that she would wear for most of the day, except during practice and competitions. Taylor repeatedly tells sports medicine staff members that she is still experiencing pain, even after months in the splint. She asks to be referred to the doctor, but, given her lack of power, nothing was done. Instead of having Taylor's complaints escalated to an administrative sports medicine staff member, they were evaded so many times that she eventually stops disclosing her pain and injuries. During our interview, Taylor explains that she felt ignored by sports medicine staff members and stopped talking to them about the pain. Eventually, Taylor told her coach about the pain. Her coach tailored her workouts and eventually her entire technique, since there were movements she could not perform because of the pain in her wrist. After two years of no care, as the pain in Taylor's wrist worsens, Taylor again complains to sports medicine staff members who gave her a steroid shot to help with the pain. Taylor says that the steroid shot did help in the short term, but the pain eventually returns. After being evaded for years, Taylor decides to express her pain and her need to be referred to a doctor to the sports medicine staff again. Four years after the initial complaint, Taylor was finally given a referral for a doctor's appointment. When Taylor finally saw a doctor, she was told that her wrist was broken. The doctor expresses that, if she had come to him when she first experienced the pain, her years of pain could have been avoided. This is an example of the way the ATC, a gendered and racialized organization, produces and reproduces a health inequity for a woman athlete of color.

## Dominant Ideologies of Gender and Nationalism

While intersectionality traditionally discusses power in relation to race and gender, nationality is a social location that can be examined, intersecting with gender, to understand discrimination in the ATC. According to Hextrum (2021), the U.S. collegiate sport system is entrenched with nationalist ideologies. International women college athletes lie at a unique intersection that affects how they navigate the U.S. collegiate sport system. In addition to experiencing sexism, this population also experiences "ethnocentrism"—a term coined by William Sumner (1906) to highlight that when one group is centered (in this case U.S. citizens) it causes other groups (international students) to be assessed in relation to them. In the market-like structure of intercollegiate athletics, both racial and ethnic minorities are being discriminated against (Newell and Sethi 2023).

Since NLU is a U.S. PWI, being an international student, specifically an international college athlete (ICA), the behavior is judged in relation to U.S.-born college athletes. In other words, domestic college athletes are centered in the ATC. However, in the ATC, international women college athletes struggle to navigate this system for a variety of reasons. The U.S. collegiate sport system is unique, and the ability to play a sport and go to school is not common in other countries. Therefore, international students come to the United States to compete and earn a degree.

The dominant ideology of nationalism is reinforced through stereotyping and can be seen in the following example. Tasha, a white international women's rowing athlete, walks up to Nancy and tells her, "My shoulder is kind of bothering me." Nancy, who is in the middle of giving Elijah, a Black men's football athlete, a flush (i.e., a massage) on his quad, asks her to take her backpack off and show her exactly where it hurts. The athlete takes off her backpack as instructed and points to a part of her back. Without physically examining the athlete (Nancy is still giving a massage to the football athlete), she explains that the issue is her scapula and that she is not using the correct technique. The athlete asks what she should do. Nancy tells her to push her shoulders down (not back) and move her neck around in circles. The athlete thanks Nancy and walks away. As soon as the athlete leaves, Nancy begins talking to Elijah about Tasha. Nancy states, "When people have never rowed before, they don't know the difference between sore and hurt." The conversation continued:

> "Who was that?" inquires Elijah. Nancy responds, "She's a freshman, foreign, I don't know where she's from I just know she has a long last name. I try not to deal with it. I will when they make the team. She's just sore."

Elijah questions what Nancy is talking about. Nancy responds, "They are just NARPS. They ask NARPS if they want to join the rowing team and then they teach them how to row."

Elijah nods his head to acknowledge he understands. NARP is a degrading acronym that stands for "non-athletic regular person." I heard this term used often in the ATC to refer to nonathletes, specifically non-NCAA athletes.

Nancy has Elijah move onto his stomach to finish his flush. As Elijah is turning, Sophie, a white international women's rowing athlete, walks over to Elijah and says, "That looks sore." Elijah looks confused. Sophie repeats her statement, slower this time, pronouncing each word, "That . . . looks . . . sore." "She's Australian," Nancy chimes in. "Is Russell Crowe a national hero there," asks Elijah. "Russell Crowe? Yeah." Sophie responds, before rolling her eyes and walking away.

## Exceptions

However, there were exceptions to this finding. For example, Maddie, a Black women's soccer athlete, had a positive healthcare experience in the ATC with her athletic trainer, David, a Black man. Maddie experienced reoccurring acute injuries throughout her time at NLU. In each instance, she discusses how attentive the athletic trainer assigned to her team, David, was. The sports medicine staff member even went so far as to call her parents to keep them updated on her rehabilitation. Ray (2019) discusses that the participation of people of color in racialized organizations either produces or challenges racial hierarchies. The sport scholar John Singer (2009) argues that in college sport, there is a need for more Black role models in leadership roles at PWIs. There is a need for challenges to the racial hierarchy, such as this example.

This section highlights issues of access to healthcare. While all athletes seemingly have access to the ATC, not all are accepted in this space because they do not align with the dominant gender and/or racial ideologies. This can be especially consequential to women of color. But, to be effective, a space must be structured to advance the health and welfare of everyone, including non-profit-generating sport athletes.

Similarly, Kate, a white women's basketball player from overseas, pays tribute to her athletic trainer during her recovery process, stating:

> She's a couple years older than I am and I always tell her you are not just an athletic trainer you are also my personal psychologist because I mean she knows me really well, and also she knows I don't talk about my feelings and everything, so she knows when I feel bad or sad, whatever it is. She knows certain things I say so, she really kept my head above water last year, so I am thankful for that.

Kate had a positive experience with her athletic trainer who also put in the effort to check on her mental health while she was going through her recovery process. Sports medicine staff, specifically athletic trainers, play a major role in providing social support to injured collegiate athletes. The sports medicine staff aid in fixing both physical and mental injuries, however, only one sports medicine staff member (i.e., the sport psychologist) is truly trained for the mental aspect.

The organization of the ATC is found to affect the sports medicine staff members with whom the athletes come into contact. In each athletic training room, there are athletic trainers and physical therapists. However, only the main athletic training room has the sport psychologist and nutritionist. The physicians are not housed in the athletic training rooms but rather in a medical facility set apart from these spaces. Given this organization, athletes are in contact with athletic training and physical therapy resources more than any other sports medicine staff members. In addition, athletic trainers act as liaisons between athletes and the other sports medicine staff. This arrangement puts a strain on athletic trainers and makes it more difficult for them to devote adequate time to each athlete because, in addition to treating injuries, they are also trying to be a source of social support for athletes.

## Conclusions

Sport is a microcosm in which race relations and gender inequities in America are perpetuated. This statement is consistent with observations in the ATC studied. The ATC possesses characteristics of a gendered and racialized organization that adversely affect women of color. Athlete healthcare upholds white supremacy and patriarchy by letting people of color and women know they will not receive the same care as others.

The findings are consistent with the view that dominant ideologies of gender and race are infused into the ATC and are perpetuated by athletes and sports medicine staff. These dominant ideologies were found to be reinforced through various mechanisms such as stereotyping and evasion. Also revealed is that these mechanisms used to reinforce the dominant ideologies have consequences for identifying injury, thereby creating health inequities, especially among women of color. Further, as a gendered and racialized organization that focuses on profit-generating sport athletes, the ATC affects the care that sports medicine staff provide and athletes receive. This difference in treatment is an effect of the NCAA, a capitalist enterprise that operates in a racialized society.

The examples provided show how the ATC socially constructs gender and race, along with the dominant ideologies of gender and race that result in health inequities. In the ATC, the meanings of gender and race are seen as absolute, when, in reality, they are socially constructed. Specifically, the ATC is a space where the understandings of gender and race are created and, therefore, people who enter this space begin to develop such understandings. Particularly noteworthy is that the structure of the ATC causes dominant ideologies to be viewed as absolute. These ideologies are adopted by athletes and sports medicine staff who then reinforce these ideologies. Therefore, new athletes and sports medicine staff who enter the space are inundated with the dominant ideology of gender and race.

Examining the mechanisms utilized to enforce the dominant ideologies of gender and race highlights their effect on everyday interactions. This finding is important because the gendered and racialized meanings of injury are learned by sports medicine staff and athletes, who then share those meanings with others outside of the ATC. However, what must be recognized is that the socially constructed gendered and racialized meanings in sport can be enforced before involvement in collegiate sport, such as in youth sport (Allison 2018; Eckstein 2017; Eitzen 2009; Hasbrook and Harris 2000). For example, the findings reveal that some athletes experienced gendered and racialized meanings of sport that pressured them to play through injuries in elementary school, middle school, and high school. For other athletes, college was the first time that this pressure to play through injury was experienced. While collegiate sport may not be the only place where this problem is prevalent, it is perpetuated. Understanding how the socially constructed concepts of gender and race affect meanings of health and injury is important so that these constructions are not inadvertently reified.

# 8

## Recognition of Injury

The NCAA utilizes a biomedical approach to injury treatment that focuses on physical processes. The biomedical approach "assumes disease to be fully accounted for by deviations from the norm of measurable biological (somatic) variables" (Engel 1977: 130). However, the utilization of a biomedical approach ignores social processes and fails to center athletes. In sport, being healthy, or able-bodied, is the norm. Norms are the informal rules that guide what people do and how they live. Norms are reinforced through sanctions. Negative sanctions are punishments, while positive sanctions are rewards. When we violate group norms, we are seen as deviant and will likely be punished. On the other hand, if we follow group norms, we will likely be rewarded. We learn what is normal through socialization, both primary (inside the home) and secondary (outside the home).

The political scientist Robert Crawford (2006) has studied the meaning of health in American culture and argues that what it means to be healthy has been created in relation to social structures. Moreover, normalcy is socially constructed (Davis 2010). The disability scholar Lennard J. Davis argues that the concept of normalcy was created during the nineteenth century and implies that most people should be part of the norm. Therefore, injury is seen as abnormal. Davis argues that to understand the disabled body, we must look at the normal body. The problem lies, in part, in the construction of what is "normal."

An additional issue is that injuries are a social construction that occurs within, and are products of, social arrangements (B. Turner and Wainwright 2003: 271). The meaning of injury has been created within the ATC. I ask a physical therapist on staff named Michael, a white Latino man, to define injury, and he responds:

> *Obviously*, injury is some type of insult, trauma, or derangement of some type of tissue, whether you are talking about physiologically or psychologically. You're dealing with any bodily system that seems different from the norm.

While obvious to Michael, this definition of injury is not so obvious to nonmedical professionals, including athletes. The meaning of injury differs from athlete to athlete. For example, Mary, an Asian international athlete on the swimming and diving team, discusses her "injury," stating:

> I'm actually not that much of an injury-prone person. I've been pretty robust. I mean I've had random bits involved but nothing that was ever actually anything serious. I remember I had a sprained rib for a while. I don't think it was that big of a deal. I don't know. I think I took a week off training, that was it. I never had to have any operation. Like, I've never had an operation for an injury.

Mary continues to discuss how she never had surgery, so she does not consider herself to have experienced an injury. While surgery is what defined an injury for Mary, another athlete, Alice, a white women's swimming and diving athlete, did not feel the same. When I asked Alice about her experience with injury, she responds:

> Luckily, I haven't had any injuries. I only tore my meniscus and posterior cruciate ligament (PCL). That was the first time I had surgery or anything, and I had to be in a full leg cast for three weeks. But that was it.

Alice downplays her injury, which required surgery, not even referring to it as an injury. All athletes gave varying definitions of injury. I attempted to further understand injury in relation to health. One day, while conducting observations in the main athletic training room, I asked Elizabeth what she thinks it means to get healthy. "For people," she pauses for a moment, then responds:

> ... *here* I think it means that the athletes want to get back on the field. They are so used to a routine that they just want to get back to practice.

What it means to be injured is contested and, to further understand the meaning of injury (non-able-bodied), we need to understand being healthy (able-bodied). Being able-bodied is also understood in relation to the ability to sell one's labor. Further, neoliberal political and economic logic are contingent on disabled bodies (McRuer 2006). Moreover, neoliberal capitalism is devastating to disabled people.

In *Crip Theory: Cultural Signs of Queerness and Disability*, the theorist Robert McRuer (2006) introduces the theory of compulsory able-bodiedness, which argues that being able-bodied is seen as the norm, therefore, being non-able-bodied (or disabled) is seen as deviant and, at times, invisible. This is because identities exist in relation to one another. However, it is important to recognize that these identities are caught up in power structures. Being able-bodied is the dominant ideology that is pushed onto us. When one identity is seen as normal, being able-bodied, other identities are marginalized (e.g., being disabled or injured). McRuer argues that compulsory able-bodiedness is intertwined with compulsory heteronormativity. Moreover, he argues that compulsory able-bodiedness and compulsory heteronormativity reinforce one another. Compulsory heteronormativity normalizes heterosexuality, thereby causing nonhetero identities to be seen as deviant.

## Biographical Disruption

According to the historian John Hoberman (1944: 2), "High-performance sport is a medically hazard activity." One medical hazard of sport is injury, which can affect collegiate athletes whose identities are intrinsically tied to their sport. An injury may cause an athlete to adjust the way they play their sport or to stop playing altogether, disrupting their biography—or what the sociologist Michael Bury (1982) calls a biographical disruption. Utilizing biographical disruption as a concept to understand injury illustrates how closely acute and chronic injuries are tied to the identities of athletes. For the athletes interviewed who experienced a biographical disruption due to an injury, their identities were intrinsically tied to their sport. In other words, these athletes had a high athletic identity. The psychologists Britton W. Brewer, Judy L. Van Raalte, and Darwyn E. Linder (1993) define athletic identity as the degree to which an individual identifies with an athletic role. For example, Ben, a white men's swimming and diving athlete, states:

> Being an [athlete] is a huge part of my life. It is kind of my identity in a sense. I have been doing it for so long and I have gotten to a certain point in my career and it's just who I am, you know.... It is just kind of who I am at this point, and it is something that I will always be.

Ben is displaying role engulfment, which occurs when a person's identification is based on the role that person assumes (i.e., an athlete). The sociologists Patricia Adler and Peter Adler (1991) examine role engulfment and the changes in college athletes' identities over the years in their book *Backboards and Blackboards*. Brianna also shows signs of role engulfment when she explains that she always puts her sport first, particularly because of her goal of making it to the Olympics. She states:

> Sport, especially now, is a big part of my personality. It has been for the last eleven years, and I don't see myself going away from it. Like I wake up every morning, everything, even school, has revolved around my sport. I shouldn't but I put my sport before schoolwork and this and that because I want to be the best I can be. So, I have goals and ambitions that I want to get to by the next Olympics cycle, and I want to be there. So, I feel like if I don't put my sport first and my ambitions, goals, thoughts, and opinions, and tell people about them and how things should

be and how I can get better, then I feel like it's all for nothing. Rowing makes me who I am.

One of the characteristics of being an athlete is the use of the body to play a specific sport. However, when athletes experience an injury and are unable to use the body to perform in their sport, this inability disrupts their biography as an athlete. This also brings the risk of subsuming to athlete identity foreclosure which is when the commitment to the athlete role is of the utmost importance and there is no exploration of alternatives (Brewer and Petitpas 2017). Since these athletes are so connected to their sport, experiencing an injury disrupts this major part of their biography and, if no other options have been explored past being an athlete, danger can ensue. For the purposes of this chapter, an acute injury is defined as an injury that is the result of a single traumatic event (e.g., a bone fracture), while a chronic injury is a result of prolonged and repetitive motions.

Bury (1982) uses the case of the chronic illness of rheumatoid arthritis to understand disruption in biography, finding that this chronic illness is a specific type of disruptive experience. When an illness is experienced, there is a disruption of behaviors (i.e., day-to-day routines) that were formerly taken for granted, causing individuals to fundamentally rethink their biography. According to Bury (1982), biographical disruption is characterized by the following three aspects: recognition, uncertainty, and the mobilization of resources.

Sport researchers have examined the effect of chronic and long-term injuries on biographical disruption (Allen-Collinson and Hockey 2007; Malcolm and Pullen 2018). For example, the sport scholars Jacquelyn Allen-Collinson and John Hockey (2007) utilized an autoethnography to examine the identity work of biographical disruption in nonelite runners, finding that identity work is a crucial component in maintaining a sport identity after the disruption caused by injury. Dominic Malcolm and Emma Pullen (2018) examined the relationship between biographical disruption and sport-related injury among nonelite sport/exercise participants, finding that there are biographical contingencies (e.g., youthfulness) that perpetuate and escalate biographical disruption. To my knowledge, no research explores biographical disruption in the context of acute and chronic injuries suffered by collegiate athletes. *A key point is that experiencing an injury is a form of biographical disruption for collegiate athletes with acute or chronic injuries.* However, the findings reveal that the degree of biographical disruption differs depending on whether the injury is acute or chronic. The following sections further examine the biographical disruption among athletes with acute injuries and chronic injuries as they pass through recognition and uncertainty.

## Recognition

Recognition of injury is the first characteristic of biographical disruption. For athletes who experience an injury, the inability to use the body as needed (i.e., for sport and/or daily tasks) is the first marker in a biographical shift. However, the experience leading up to this condition differed between those who experienced acute injuries and those who suffered chronic injuries.

## Recognition of Acute Injury

For athletes with acute injuries, the injury resulted from a sudden event, and their inability to use the body was recognized almost immediately (one to two days). Athletes who suffer an acute injury sometimes do not experience pain; rather the injury manifests as an inability to use the body. This sequence differs from Bury (1982), who found chronic illness to be associated with the onset of pain and suffering.

Mark, a white Latino men's baseball athlete, explains that his injury occurred when he fell while running for a ball. He explains, "I was not in pain, just my leg was swollen. I had to ice the whole night." Mark continued that he could not bend his knee or walk and needed crutches for assistance. This inability to use the body is what caused him to realize that he was injured. Similarly, Maddie, a Black women's soccer athlete, states:

> It wasn't till the next day where I literally woke up and my knee was so swollen and I couldn't walk, so we knew something was wrong.

Maddie did not experience pain but rather her injury impaired her ability to walk unaided, which is when she recognized that she was injured.

## Recognition of Chronic Injury

In sport, pain and injury are normalized through what Howard Nixon (1993, 1994) calls the "culture of risk" and "biased social support" that can influence messages that normalize experiences of injury. Pain in sport is normalized in expressions such as "no pain, no gain" and "feel the burn," indicating that pain is a positive attribute that is associated with progress. Due to this culture, many athletes will play until they are physically unable to continue. This behavior was especially the case among athletes with chronic injuries. In some instances, athletes with chronic injuries played with prolonged pain in the belief that they were getting stronger. It was not until they felt that something was "wrong" that they sought help. For example, Ben, a white men's swimming and diving athlete, discusses feeling pain but playing through the discomfort. He states:

> I noticed a little bit of pain in my [body] but just kind of seemed like I may have overworked it a little bit, so we took a little rest and then it was fine then I came back, and I did a certain [move] one day, I [moved] too hard and it was kind of hard to bend over and walk so I went to the training room and got some X-rays and MRIs and found out I [was injured].

Even though many athletes experienced pain, for some, not until they believed something was "wrong" and they were unable to use their body to its fullest did they consider themselves to be injured. Joni, a white international women's golf athlete, explains this outlook well, stating that "for me being injured was the type of pain that I felt when I started realizing that something was wrong." These feelings of something being wrong occurred during different activities, some sport related and others not. For example, Jennifer, a white international women's swimming and diving athlete, discusses having pain for months. Then, at practice, something changed, which she described as, "I could feel something was wrong." She continued by explaining that parts of her body did not seem stable when she was engaging in her sport. Emily, a white women's basketball athlete, also realized that she was injured during practice:

> [The injury] happened over time but there was that last instant when I jumped that I really felt it when it made me realize there was really something wrong.

For others, this recognition of injury and something being wrong occurred outside of their sport when the body was unable to perform seemingly normal activities. For example, Ashley, a white Hispanic women's tennis athlete and international student, explained that daily activities such as picking up her phone would bother her, and, "at that point, I knew there was something wrong." In these instances, injury is not defined by pain but rather by a change in the athletes' physical ability to go about their everyday lives. Moreover, in these instances, injury caused the athletes' embodied orientation to the world to change. For athletes, pain is tolerated as long as their physical functioning in their sport and/or daily life is not severely impacted. When the athletes were no longer able to physically function, they then deemed themselves injured.

A caveat of biographical disruption is when illness or injury is expected. For those who expect to experience a chronic illness, there is a limited disruption in their biography. Moreover, for some athletes, injury is an anticipated rather than disruptive event; therefore, injury is a form of biographical reinforcement (Carricaburu and Pierret 1995), meaning that experiencing an injury made the athletes' identity even stronger since the injury was anticipated. The *NCAA Sports Medicine Handbook* (2014: 4) states, "Participation in intercollegiate athletics involves unavoidable exposure to an inherent risk of injury." I ask each interviewee if they thought college sport involved inherent risk and found that this idea that sport involves an inherent risk is believed by some but not all. Diane, a white international women's tennis athlete, agreed, stating, "I feel like in sports it's definitely normal to have these injuries and deal with them."

Similarly, after a forty-five-minute interview with Jennifer, a white international women's swimming and diving athlete, talking about a horrific injury she experienced, I express my regret for everything that she has gone through with her injury. She responds with saying, "No, it's just part of it. It's part of it, unfortunately." Rationalization such as this was common among athletes who often refer to their injuries as "part of the game" (Curry 1993; Weber [1904] 1958). Some athletes claim that pain contributes to the development of "character," which allows them to gain the respect of others immersed in the sport world. While athletes are not forced to play hurt, external and internal factors lead many athletes to choose to play when they are injured.

Sociologists have focused on the meaning of sport injury from the perspectives of coaches, athletes, athletic trainers, physical therapists, doctors, and the media. In the early 1990s, James Frey discussed the rise of risk research in the sociology of sport, post–James F. Short's 1984 presidential address at the American Sociological Association (ASA) meeting, and subsequent publication of "The Social Fabric at Risk" (Short 1984; Frey 1991). Nixon (1993) extended this discussion by addressing the "culture of risk" in sport. Through a content analysis of *Sports Illustrated* articles, Nixon (1993) examined the dominant cultural themes about sport. Nixon described one of the themes as the socialization of athletes through which they learn and internalize expected behavior, roles, beliefs, and feelings. Nixon found that athletes are socialized to adopt a specific set of beliefs about risk and pain. More specifically, athletes minimized or ignored injuries and pain and learned to play hurt. In doing this, the pain and injury experience is normalized.

While the notion that injury is part of the game is believed by athletes, not all athletes think that injury will happen to them. For example, Matthew, a white men's football athlete, states:

> The more you play, you're more likely to get hurt or tweak something every now and then. But, no, I don't think I expected to have three ACL tears.

In this instance, Matthew is breaking away from what Nixon (1993) calls the "culture of risk" and challenges the notion that pain and injury is normal. However, not all feel that injury is inherent. When I asked William about this, he responded:

Well, I mean, I think the short answer is yes, right? Sport is not risk-free and depending upon the sport, there's different kinds of injuries that are . . . I don't want to say that they're inherent to that sport, but you do carry an increased risk, right?

What happens when an athlete does experience an "inherent" injury but uncertainty surrounds it? Chapters 9 and 10 explore this question in accordance with Bury's concept of biographical disruption to examine the disruption that injury causes in collegiate athletes' biographies.

# 9

# Uncertainty of Injury

For some athletes who experienced a biographical disruption from an injury, they describe the uncertainty surrounding the injury. According to Bury (1982), the uncertainty occurs when those injured have little to no idea what is happening, and it can be understood in physical and cognitive terms.

## Uncertainty of Acute Injury

Athletes who suffered acute injuries generally understood almost immediately that they had been physically injured but experienced uncertainty in their mindset over how to deal with it. For example, some athletes used the injury as motivation to get back to their sport, while others saw it as a barrier. For example, Julian, a Black Latino men's baseball athlete, experienced an acute injury during the offseason but believed he could land a starting position in season. Julian states, "I was in a good place to start so I wanted to get back as quick as possible." For those athletes who wanted to return to their sport, this motivation is derived from the desire to play. This perspective was found across all sport types.

Similarly, Amanda, a white Latina women's volleyball athlete, who was injured in her senior year with plans to graduate and start her career, explained that she did not feel as though she could take her time to get better because this was her last year to play. She states:

> I really just want to even play in practice. It doesn't matter, but I just want to be able to participate to some degree.

Differing from these reactions, some athletes were devastated by their injury. For these athletes, an injury was overwhelming. For example, as Michelle, a Black women's track-and-field athlete, declared:

> I was nervous [about competing] but moved forward. Then the injury happened, and it was like okay we are at a complete standstill. I remember talking to my mentor and telling her I hate [this sport], I don't want to do this anymore, it is too much work. Yeah, everything just kind of went down the drain. I was like I want to leave here; I don't want to be here anymore. It was just a lot going on.

Michelle experienced a concussion and saw this injury as a barrier to play, and, in the beginning, she had difficulty with her recovery process.

Athletes with acute injuries also experienced uncertainty with their first episode. For example, Julian, a Black Latino men's baseball athlete, lamented, "I was shocked to get hurt. Considering up until that point, that was the first time I had gotten hurt. I was always pretty much healthy all the time playing." Similarly, Joe, a Black men's track-and-field athlete, states that he had "a little bit of problems with [my body], but I didn't think it would cause me to have an injury." Uncertainty also arose from the definition of injury. For example, during his interview, Ray took significant time to discuss an injury he experienced, including his initial description that this event was an injury. But, later, he states, "I guess it's not really an injury. . . . I was out for two weeks, but I'm back now."

## Uncertainty of Chronic Injury

Athletes with chronic injuries often feel something is problematic with their bodies but may have little to no idea what is actually wrong. This uncertainty, or unknown, may lead to a series of appointments with physicians to diagnose their injury. However, throughout each journey, many athletes were misdiagnosed, while others remain undiagnosed. This ambiguity contributes to further disruption for athletes since the body is needed to perform their sport, which is tied to their identity. For example, Sam, a white international men's tennis athlete, confided:

> In my case, there was no diagnosis whatsoever. So, in that case, there is no structure and no guidance at all. So, there is no room for even doctor communication, at that point.

Uncertainty also occurred regarding the length of time an athlete was out even when they had a diagnosis. As Emily, a white women's basketball athlete, states:

> Well, when the injury happened, like I said, I didn't think much of it, I didn't think it was a big deal. I thought it was just something I was going to be out for a couple weeks for, but when I found out I was going to be out for the whole year I was obviously super upset and like I said it was unexpected because I have never been through something like this before but I kind of mentally was down. I was really upset about it.

For athletes who were out for an extended period of time due to their injury, they had to "re-story" the self (Malcolm and Pullen 2018), which involves the negotiation and renegotiation of identity, serving as an avenue of coping given the biographical disruption. For example, Tim, a Black international men's basketball athlete, recognizes:

> The thing about getting hurt (like when I got hurt this year) is because I couldn't play [my sport], you'd have to find what else about yourself that you like doing.

In a similar fashion, Sam discusses doing all he could to get clarification about his injury and prognosis but changing his mindset about his injury helps him the most. Sam states:

Some injuries truly are what they are, but I think just the mindset change, one, helped me take care of the details and, two, helped me play through some amount of pain that I normally would've maybe misjudged as too painful to play, or whatever. It helped me put things in the right perspective, and ultimately playing through the correct amount of pain was what helped me get back to where I needed to be.

However, for some athletes, changing your mindset is not enough. It is how others treat you that can also affect the experience. For example, Matthew, a white men's football athlete, discusses his experience after multiple injuries. He remarks:

It's nice when you're not forgotten about when you're an athlete that's injured. And more so having that coach that almost comes up to you and says "I haven't forgotten about you," once in a while. Because for me, that was nice the first time around and the second time around, but the third time I never got that. I was like, "Wow, I guess they actually forgot about me." That's not justified by saying, oh you're still in [gear], dressing out, coming to practice.

Matthew discusses feeling alienated from his coaches and team after he experienced an injury at NLU for the third time.[1] Matthew continues by discussing how even though he could not practice, he was required by the coaches to dress and be present at all practices. He discusses how at these practices, on the sidelines, injured athletes would do exercises that he describes as, "dumb things outside like riding the bike while the sun is beating down on you, riding for a half an hour. And then you'd do a little arm workout." He continues:

I don't have any problem working out, believe me, but they have guys in full pads that are hurt, not going to play, and it just

---

1. According to Marx (1844), there are four basic components of alienation. First, workers are alienated from their productive activity. Second, workers are alienated from the product. Third, workers are alienated from other workers. And fourth, workers are alienated from their own human potential.

doesn't make sense. I guess the whole thought process behind it is that you want to keep things more team oriented, making him still feel like he's more part of the team. From my aspect, I've done it three different times and hated putting on my full uniform when I knew I wasn't going to practice. I hated having to do really dumb workouts when I could've been focusing on my rehab in the meantime.

In addition to feeling alienated after his third injury, he was frustrated by the performative dressing in full gear for practice that was mandated when he believed he could have taken that time to do things that were specific for rehabilitating his injury. Instead of using that time efficiently, he had to find other time in the day with his busy schedule to come to the ATC for rehabilitation. This only furthered his uncertainty of getting back on the field.

Uncertainty can also be understood in an athlete's unknown of what is next after experiencing a career-ending injury. This is highlighted in the following example of Jack. Jack was experiencing back pain and explained to me that he knew he was hurt for some time, but he wanted to play so he kept this issue "under wraps." Once the pain became unbearable, he disclosed the injury to the sports medicine staff. He immediately got a magnetic resonance imaging (MRI) test and a computerized tomography (CT) scan the same day. The results of the tests showed that he had a spinal cord injury. Jack explained that he was taken to an administrative staff member's personal home that night and questioned if he was really hurt. Jack was confused given the results of the MRI test and a CT scan. He felt that the sports medicine staff were trying to coerce him into playing in the upcoming game against a higher-ranked team. Jack ended up playing in the upcoming game only to stop less than halfway through the game. Coercion is conceptualized as compelling someone to do something. This game would be the last that Jack ever played.

I ask Jack what his relationship is with the sports medicine staff after he sat out the rest of the season, and he explains that, from then on, he felt excluded. He believed that he was no longer given the time or level of treatment he was previously given when he was still playing. Athletes who are unable to play are entitled to receive the same level of care from sports medicine staff that was provided prior to their injuries, per NCAA guidelines on permanent total disability (PTD) coverage (NCAA 2021b). In addition to coercion, Jack experienced exclusion from the ATC. In this instance, exclusion is conceptualized as feeling unwelcome in the ATC organization. In this example, Jack was no longer of use to the university when he was unable to perform. When the body of a profit-generating sport athlete is no longer able-bodied, or useful to the university, they are excluded from the organization. NLU and the ATC have a power that is important to understand because profit-generating sport athletes with career-ending injuries are not of use to the university.

# 10

## Mobilizing Resources for Injury

The neoliberal model of the university acts as what the sociologists Bruce Link and Jo Phelan (1995) call a structural determinant of health. This is because the structure of athletics within the NLU—oriented toward profit motivation—affects the care that college athletes receive when injured.

The structural determinants and conditions in which people live and work affect their health (Marmot 2005), which, in turn, helps explain why some people are healthier than others. One of these structural determinants has to do with the resources "available." The neoliberal model creates the facade that all athletes have the opportunity to receive the same care in the ATC, however, some are able to mobilize resources for their injuries easier than others. This is the third, and final, characteristic of biographical disruption, the ability to mobilize resources.

### Mobilizing Resources for Acute Injury

For athletes with single acute injuries and reoccurring acute injuries, mobilizing resources in the ATC was easier since the injury happened suddenly, usually at a practice or game where sports medicine staff were present and a set treatment plan was created. For example, Rachel, a white women's cross-country/track-and-field athlete, discusses being injured in practice when her athletic trainer was present. After her injury occurred, she was in constant contact with the sports medicine staff and received a concrete plan of treatment.

Athletes with reoccurring acute injuries were also able to easily mobilize resources in the ATC. However, there is a stigma associated with being injured multiple times that affects relationships with others in the sport community (Goffman 1963). According to Goffman (1963: 3), "stigma" is defined as "an attribute that is deeply discrediting." For example, Jackie, a white Latina women's soccer athlete, experienced multiple acute injuries during her time as a collegiate athlete. She relayed that her coaches were supportive the first two times when she was undergoing rehabilitation; however, she states, "The third time [the coaches] looked at me differently."

## Mobilizing Resources for Chronic Injury

Athletes with chronic injuries discuss constantly managing the pain resulting from their injury, which required the regular mobilization of resources in the ATC. However, some resources were more accessible than others. For example, obtaining a bag of ice or heat is easier than getting an appointment to see an athletic trainer, which itself is easier than getting an appointment with a physician.

Observations and interviews with injured athletes revealed that pain management was employed in an effort to manage injuries so as to keep the athlete playing. (On occasion, sports medicine staff members gave advice to athletes to enable them to manage pain to keep playing.) The sports medicine staff members were also a major resource to aid in pain management. For example, the sports medicine staff provide treatment plans with various exercises to help athletes strengthen the injured body part and reduce pain. Examples of ways in which athletes managed pain were through ice (bags and baths), heat, STIM, ultrasound, manual therapy, therapeutic exercises, pain relief injections (e.g., steroid shots, Toradol shots), and pain relief medications (e.g., anti-inflammatories).

Kyle, an Indigenous Latino men's football athlete, discusses the chronic pain in his foot and that he would have to get "shots" before every game. When I inquired further to find out what shot he was referring to, he responded:

> Toradol. Toradol shot. It's for pain. So, it's supposed to take the pain away, but it didn't. It was a needle shot I got on my butt. So, I would get that every game for the pain. While also taking Pain-Off, the pill, because it was that bad.

For all athletes with chronic injuries, pain management was routinized (Morden, Jinks, and Ong 2015) and normalized. For example, Diane, a white international women's tennis athlete, states:

> At this point, I think I've mastered [managing my injuries], but I definitely don't want to get injured again because just having been injured a couple of times, it's the worst.

Similarly, athletic trainer James discusses how everyone experiences pain; however, the reaction to pain differs by person. James notes, "You have to find ways to lessen the pain."

Jennifer, a white international women's swimming and diving athlete, discusses managing a chronic injury she has had for over a year so that she could train for and compete at a major tournament. For Jennifer, the idea of "managing injuries" was introduced by the sports medicine staff. For example, Jennifer discusses interactions with staff who explained to her that her injury could be "managed" so that she could continue to play and could compete at an upcoming event. She recounted this interaction as follows:

> And then this is what really surprised me, the [sports medicine staff] were like well we could just rehab you until after the [major tournament] next year because it could be manageable.

Jennifer noted that she was the one who had to advocate for herself to stop playing even when she felt pressure from the sports medicine staff members. This idea of "managing injuries" is similar to Bury's (1982) notion of managing a chronic disease. In Bury's work, he discusses how participants "managed" or "coped" with their chronic disease, trying their best to keep it at bay or from getting worse.

Another athlete, Joni, a white international women's golfer, explained that she trains to compete at the highest level that her body can manage given her chronic injury. In her terms:

> Every year I just break my body down, and then I have to build it back up to this [manageable] point. And then I break it down.

Joni continues to explain that the breaking down and building back up of her body is possible mainly through her own group of sports medicine providers back home. Specifically, Joni went to a physical therapist at home after a recommendation from her national team coach. She noted that her injury was not improving even after going to the ATC for years. She believes it is partially because every year she had a new athletic trainer who had to learn (again) the issues she is dealing with. She states:

> It's sad that I've had to work on the same injury, but now I've just been in contact with a personal trainer to get somebody that's not related to [NLU] at all to work with me on specific training.

Jocelyn, a white international women's rowing athlete, discusses an injury she experienced at the beginning of the semester. She eventually had an appointment with a pain management specialist, but this meeting kept being pushed back, and she was not seen until the end of the semester. While she waited to see the specialist, the sports medicine staff gave Jocelyn the choice to keep playing. What Jocelyn states is interesting:

> I always heard, "It's on you. It's on you if you want to keep going or if you don't." So, [the sports medicine staff] made me decide basically if [the pain] was tolerable, or not.

While Jocelyn had to determine for herself if the injury caused her enough pain to keep playing or not, Jack noted that after he was diagnosed with a chronic injury, he did not feel welcome in the ATC:

> I can tell they really don't care, but they're going to say, act, and try to do the right things. I wasn't born yesterday. Maybe it's

me, but I can sense it. I can sense the disappointment, what could've been, you know.

Jack says that he feels pressure from the sports medicine staff to perform, and when he is deemed unable to play because of a chronic injury he felt forgotten. When athlete bodies can no longer be used for sport purposes, they are viewed differently and, in some cases, abandoned.

Athletes with undiagnosed and misdiagnosed chronic injuries had more difficulty mobilizing resources in the ATC, because of the stigmatization associated with chronic injuries (Goffman 1963). This finding is similar to Bury's (1982), who found that when there is a stigma associated with a chronic illness, mobilizing resources is difficult. This stigmatization arises from the ambivalence surrounding definitions of chronicity, pain, and injury. According to Bury (1982: 172), access to medical knowledge "offers an opportunity to conceptualize the disease as separate from the individual's self." Moreover, access to medical knowledge allows athletes to understand the disease outside of themselves.

While the meanings of these concepts are subjective, the sports medicine staff and athletes utilizing the ATC tend to see them as objective. This disconnect is exacerbated because the meanings of pain and injury differ within the sport community and even among the sports medicine staff. Moreover, there is a dichotomy between pain and functioning. The change in embodied orientation—athletes' abilities to engage normatively with the world—is paramount to subjective pain. However, this dichotomy affects mobilizing resources; those who are undiagnosed or misdiagnosed have difficulty mobilizing resources and receiving care. For example, Lily, although she experienced what she described as unbearable pain, was not cleared to miss practice. Therefore, she continued to play through the pain. Lily had a series of doctor's appointments but no diagnosis of an injury. Nonetheless, Lily voiced to the sports medicine staff that something was not right with her body, resulting in a series of misdiagnoses. Since Lily was still able to use her body to play her sport, the pain she was experiencing was downplayed.

The scholars José Pena-López and José Sánchez-Santos (2017) argue that social capital plays a role in the mobilization of resources.

The networks athletes have allow them to mobilize resources, or not. While multiple athletes discuss injuries that are to the point of being no longer able-bodied, such as not being able to walk, their resources differed. For example, profit-generating sport athletes who were unable to walk were driven around on golf carts. Tim, a Black athlete from outside the United States in a profit-generating sport explains his experience with being carted around campus. He explains how his coaches organize everything to make sure he is picked up to be brought to class and practice on time, and someone is waiting with the golf cart when the class is over. This was not the same for all athletes, though. When asked about getting a ride on a golf cart when she was unable to walk, Jocelyn, a white international women's rowing athlete exclaims:

> Oh no, they wouldn't do that for me. . . . I didn't even have a scooter. . . . I didn't feel I was in a place to say something very demanding [like ask for a ride on the golf cart].

Those who lack the social capital associated with being a profit-generating sport athlete struggle to mobilize other resources, even if they are seemingly available to all. For example, Isabella, a white Latina women's soccer athlete, discusses how she was not comfortable utilizing the sport psychologist. She states:

> They always say oh you can talk to [the sport psychologist] and everything, but at that point, I just didn't feel comfortable. It's something that I definitely need to work on because it does help speaking to someone about it sometimes just to kind of rant get it out of your body but at the time, I was new I didn't really know anyone I just didn't feel comfortable enough just to go up to someone and be like "hey this is what I'm going through and I'm feeling all these emotions."

Not only does Isabella not feel comfortable talking to the sport psychologist; she does not even feel comfortable asking the undergraduate athletic training students for help. She states:

> I don't feel confident enough to ask one of the assistants who's still in that training, you know?

This phenomenon of being unable to communicate is similar to the sociologist Faye Wachs's (2023: 127) concept of "social disability," which "impacts an individual's ability to communicate with self and others, especially in social settings." But, for Isabella, this disability comes from a feeling of social division and lack of entitlement to the resources that are surely there for someone else. This inability to communicate acts as a barrier for athletes to mobilize resources care for an injury.

The sports medicine staff members also played a role in how athletes mobilized resources, teaching them not to use too much. For example, the sports medicine staff members continuously talked about how they want athletes to be aware of their bodies. In this regard, physical therapist Michael, a white Latino man, states:

> Ideally, I want [athletes] to be autonomous.... Each day would be a little different, depending on what they're here for, but ideally, after the first few weeks, we're working and progressing to get back to sport and have them truly be autonomous, independent, and able to do everything we ask of them.

Thus, athletes are conscripted into the profit model of the institution, seeing their care not as the objective of the department but as a drag on resources that detracts from its neoliberal objectives. Michael explains that when athletes come in as freshmen, he teaches them what is needed in their first few weeks and then expects them to be autonomous, or independent, after that. Similarly, athletic trainer Maria states:

> Helping teach that kinesthetic awareness is part of our job as well. I don't want my athletes to depend on me. I want my athletes to come in and say, "alright I'm sure I need to do a recovery device." Or "I'm sore I need to get in the tub." "I'm sore, I need Normatec boots." Or whatever. Versus having an athlete come in and say, "when I do this movement or this task, I have pain here. And I don't have pain here when I do other tasks."

While this idea of autonomy is good, there are issues in place with this because of the structure of the organization that is created by neoliberalism. In the neoliberal model, deregulation—reducing or eliminating the role of the organizing body—then places the responsibility onto others. The NCAA has already done this by pushing the responsibility of healthcare onto the universities. The sports medicine staff members of the universities are then trying to put the responsibility of health onto the athletes. To some sports medicine staff members, athletes are in control of their care. However, not all athletes have the ability to take control of their care given the unequal power dynamic in the ATC.

In observed interactions when athletes try to be "autonomous" and attempt to do something on their own, they are spoken to in demoralizing ways. For example, an athletic trainer, Katie watches as Anthony, a Black men's cross-country/track-and-field athlete, walks to the hydrocollator to get a heat pack, wraps his arm, and sits down at a training table. Katie then proceeds to yell at Anthony from across the athletic training room:

WHY ARE YOU HEATING YOUR ARM? WHY ARE YOU HEATING YOUR ARM? YOU... ARE... WARM.

Anthony, who has just come from practice, takes off the heat pack, puts it back in the hydrocollator, and leaves the athletic training room. Katie watches again and rolls her eyes. When Anthony attempts to be autonomous, he is criticized but not given the correct answer of how to help himself.

In another example, athletic trainer Noah reads aloud an email from his phone that he received from the NCAA, "If you could change one thing about the approach to concussion in sports, what would you change?" His colleague Brian, replies, "It's hard to say because everyone is different." Noah says, "I don't think we need to make a change. The athlete needs to communicate to us." Brian nods his head in agreement. This places the responsibility for athlete care on the athlete, even as experience shows athletes that the training staff often doubts them and undermines their authority over their care.

While autonomy may be one of the goals, given the dominant ideologies in the ATC (masculinity and whiteness) and neoliberalism, some athletes have the ability to mobilize resources better than others. In other words, the structure of the ATC affects the ability of athletes to utilize their agency to get care. Moreover, neoliberal discourse, such as the use of the narrative "autonomous," is entrenched in the ATC, which affects athletes' ability to get healthy.

## Conclusions

Biographical disruption was not found to operate in the same way for acute and chronic injuries. While athletes found both acute and chronic injuries to be disruptive, the disruptions were experienced in different ways. Athletes recognized they were injured when they were unable to use their bodies to perform their sport. However, this recognition was different for athletes with acute injuries as contrasted with athletes with chronic injuries. While athletes who experienced acute and chronic injuries recognized them when they were unable to use their bodies, those with acute injuries did not necessarily experience pain. Athletes with chronic injuries, on the other hand, played through the pain until they realized something was "wrong" and the pain affected their performance.

In terms of uncertainty, both athletes with acute injuries and athletes with chronic injuries experienced uncertainties surrounding injury. However, this uncertainty was more pronounced among athletes with undiagnosed or misdiagnosed chronic injuries. Athletes with chronic injuries that are undiagnosed or misdiagnosed have a difficult time mobilizing resources because of the uncertainty of the injury, while athletes with reoccurring acute injuries also have a difficult time mobilizing resources, which is perceived to be due to the stigma associated with someone who is repeatedly injured. Finally, the inability to mobilize resources was found to cause a prolonged disruption in biography, especially for athletes with reoccurring acute injuries and undiagnosed and misdiagnosed chronic injuries.

College sport operates as a system. This system is expected to work without glitches. Athletes who are injured are deemed broken and are glitches, which affects their ability to work in the system. The point is that the institutionalized system of collegiate athletics heightens the risk of biographical disruption of injury for athletes. An interesting question is whether the biographical disruption that occurs is similar for both athletes in the NCAA and those who compete independently outside of this U.S. collegiate sport system.

The ATC acts as a space to quickly fix injuries. The ATC has proven to be highly capable of fixing acute injuries; however, fixing chronic injuries was found to be more difficult. Further, when athletes experience an injury, they have to restructure their days to include rehabilitation. This accommodation affects the amount of time they interact with teammates and coaches, as they often miss practices or games. Therefore, sports medicine staff act as the main sources of social support for many athletes who experience an injury. While this study examined the role of sports medicine staff in biographical disruption, future research should examine the role of social support from the sport community (i.e., coaches, teammates, and fans) in the biographical disruption.

# Conclusion

It is 6:10 A.M., and I walk into the main athletic training room and put my backpack down in front of John's office, like I do every time I conduct observations (per his suggestion). I take out my notebook and pen and walk to the far end of the athletic training room by table six. I watch intently and take notes for the next hour and a half, not talking to anyone. At 7:40 A.M., Noah waves to me with his fingertips from across the athletic training room. He walks over to the sink, close to where I am sitting. "Good morning!" he says enthusiastically. "Good morning," I say. "How's your diary?" "It's great," I respond politely. Comments to me like this became the norm in the main athletic training room. On a different day, I walk to put my school bag down in front of John's office, like I did every time, and when I turn around, John is right there, "I thought someone was loitering in front of my office, but it's just you," he says.

Eventually, my access to the ATC was revoked. I used a magnetized card to enter the facility, and my card stopped working. When I asked about getting my card re-magnetized, I was told I needed to have an appointment with a sports medicine staff member to enter the ATC. I emailed multiple sports medicine staff members and never heard back.

This interaction highlights the gatekeeping in the collegiate sport community and is an example of the institutionalization of college athletes in the total institution of the U.S. collegiate sport system. The sport scholars Michael Giardina and Joshua Newman (2014) describe this to be part of the politics involved in research. However, Canada and colleagues (2022) argue for the need for sport researchers to gain access to the population of college athletes to improve their situation. However, gatekeeping such as the example mentioned in the previous paragraph makes this difficult.

## Advancing the Study of the Sociology of Sport

In this book, I have reviewed key sociological perspectives on race, gender, and health using the case of sport. The major findings from this study reveal the negative effect of capitalism and neoliberal logic on college athlete healthcare.

The current study adds to the sociology of sport and medical sociology literature on injury by improving the understanding of athlete injury in sport institutions, in terms of injury behaviors, perspectives of injury, and the culture of risk (Nixon 1993). The findings reveal that injury behaviors differ depending on whether injuries are acute or chronic, as noted in biographical disruption theory (Bury 1982). Athletes with one acute injury had little disruption to their biography, compared to athletes with chronic injuries or with reoccurring acute injuries. Relatedly, the findings reveal that athletes' perspectives of injury vary given the degree of biographical disruption. According to the literature, there are gendered responses to injury, and the current study found that mechanisms such as evasion and silencing were utilized to reinforce these gendered responses to pain in this gendered organization. In the ATC, profit-generating sport athletes were seen as masculine, and the injuries of those who played non-profit-generating sports were often compared to them. Moreover, sports medicine staff members embodied these ideals surrounding injury, and athletes were found to internalize and even force them onto other athletes. Given this scenario, these gendered and racialized responses to injury are social constructions imposed by the organization of the ATC (Berger and Luckmann 1966).

Moreover, the NCAA capitalizes on the culture of risk and the normalization of pain and injury (Nixon 1993). The current study reveals that for the most part, athletes have internalized the behavior, roles, beliefs, and feelings that surround injury. The phenomena that pertain to injury center on the dominant gender and racial ideologies. For example, men athletes were found to compare their injuries to profit-generating masculine sport athlete injuries, while women athletes were found to compare their injuries to any men's sport athlete injuries. In addition, sports medicine staff members also compared other athletes' injuries to the masculine profit-generating sport athletes' injuries.

## What Next?

Sport communities are often talked of as "families," and, while the underlying intention is good, the capitalist aspect of it corrupts character and how people in this space are treated. For example, many sports medicine staff members I talked to love their job and want the best for athletes. If we take this mentality and remove the economic system, we could really have life in "community."

Capitalism, the economic and political system in the United States, enables athletes to be commodified. Moreover, capitalism allows athletes to be exploited and taken advantage of. The conditions in which college athletes find themselves must be improved, specifically regarding their healthcare. Athletes who are injured (physically and mentally) while playing college sport should be entitled to a lifetime of services to cover the care needed. Gaston Gayles and colleagues (2018) argues that the current policies and practices of the NCAA disenfranchise vulnerable populations, therefore, reform structures that are supportive, equitable, and inclusive must be put in place. The following sections provide suggestions for reforms to the NCAA, member institutions, the sports medicine discipline, and athletes.

## Reforms to the NCAA

The *NCAA Sports Medicine Handbook* (2014: 4) identifies, among its goals, minimizing the risks of injury from participation in athletics.

Attainment of this goal is achieved by providing the same guidelines and standards to everyone involved. Further, the NCAA (2020) is self-described as a "member-led organization dedicated to the well-being and lifelong success of college athletes"; however, the perception of injured athletes is that the ATC does not live up to this promise. Revealed in this study is that a primary goal of the ATC is to generate profit, which can best be done by quickly "fixing" athlete injuries in furtherance of the ongoing success of the sport team and the perceived success of the athletic department. In this regard, the ATC appears less concerned with the lifelong success of athletes who have suffered injury. These findings have implications for the inclusion of athletes in discussions and decision-making concerning injury.

While the inclusion of athlete voices at recent NCAA conferences appears to be a new trend, this change does not seem to have extended to an intense focus on athlete injury. The Student-Athlete Advisory Committee (SAAC) is one representative of students that allows athletes to have a voice in the NCAA through their membership in committees on campus, in conferences, and at the national level (NCAA 2019a). However, the inclusion of athletes who experience injury should also be part of the NCAA, given the importance of injury and care.

The findings of this study also imply a need to adjust the organization of the ATC given the priorities of the NCAA. If the NCAA is dedicated to the well-being and lifelong success of college athletes, then dealing with the enduring effects of injury should receive greater attention. This suggestion means that all athletes should receive the same care regardless of their sport and regardless of whether the athlete is able to return to play.

## Reforms to NCAA Member Institutions

Although the NCAA (2014) provides guidelines under which ATCs operate at universities, member institutions retain significant autonomy. The NCAA (2014: 2) states that "determination of appropriate care and treatment of student-athletes must be based on clinical judgment of the institution's team physician or athletic healthcare team that is consistent with sound principles of sports medicine care." Therefore, the member institutions should regularly review ATCs. In such a review, members outside of the university that are part of the ACSM could undertake observations in the ATC and interview the sports medicine staff and the athletes who utilize the ATC to examine the climate of the organization (Newcomer, Hatry, and Wholey 2015). Following these reviews, a report should be made publicly available. In making these reports publicly available, all will have access, including those who have a vested interest such as the athletic administration and the president of the university.

## Reforms to the Sports Medicine Discipline

The expertise of practitioners in this field has long been taken for granted by athletes in intercollegiate athletics, in part, because sports medicine has become increasingly institutionalized through the establishment of the NCAA (Goffman 1961). The ACSM was created in response to injuries in collegiate sports to maintain health at the national level (ACSM 2023). However, this organization is disproportionately focused on physical health and the biomedical model. Exclusive reliance on a biomedical approach ignores the social processes and lived experiences of collegiate athletes (Barbour 1995). Utilizing athletes' perspectives on injury, the current study highlights the need for psychosocial training in the sports medicine discipline. This psychosocial training will incorporate psychology, sociology, and social work to provide a more holistic understanding of health and injury (Engel 1977).

Since athletic trainers are stretched thin, perhaps more social support specialists (e.g., sport psychologists, sport social workers, life coaches) should be added to the ATC. There is only one sport psychologist for the entire ATC studied. Incorporating more sport psychologists will be beneficial to the athletes. Additionally, sport social workers and sport sociologists could provide insight into the sociocultural aspects of athlete injuries in ATCs. By providing various social support specialists, a more holistic space can be maintained. Another beneficial change to the sports medicine discipline would be adding in more social science components to the continuing education units that sports medicine staff members are already required to complete.

## Reforms to Athletes

The sport scholars Kenneth Shropshire and Collin Williams (2017), in *The Miseducation of the Student Athlete*, build on Shropshire's Sports Power Matrix, which is a way to examine the power that exists in sport. They show that the NCAA has the largest amount of power, followed by Presidents and Conference Commissioners and Athletic Administrators, then college athletes, and, last, various external stakeholders. However, they argue that athletes have more power than they believe. Similarly, while athletes are often discussed as powerless, Eddie Comeaux (2017) argues that current athletes and their advocates hold an extreme amount of power. According to Marx (1844), if athletes come to the realization that they are all workers and band together, change can occur.

This can happen, in part, through the help of sport scholars. The scholar-activist H. Edwards, who served as a consultant for various professional sport organizations, also helped create the Olympic Project for Human Rights (OPHR) with athlete-activists Tommie Smith and John Carlos, which was centered on human rights for Black folk in the United States and abroad. On the podium at the 1968 Olympics, Smith and Carlos engaged in the Black Power salute to protest racial injustices around the world and in sport. According to H. Edwards, critical sport scholars can use their knowledge and mentor athletes to make change. As Zirin (2011: 219) writes, "The next Smith/Carlos moment is there for any student-athletes willing to grasp it."

The mindset of an athlete tends to perpetuate the narrative that young adults have to fight through their injuries to be successful and part of the team, which is pushed onto them by those in the sport community. Athletes who are afraid to disrupt their identity are more likely to keep quiet when they are injured. To make sure athletes are taken care of and healthy, they should be offered other outlets to disclose injuries (physical and mental). Therefore, having other practitioners in this space will allow all athletes to be fully supported.

The importance of healthy relationships should also be emphasized in discussions between athletes, sports medicine staff, and coaches. In addition, athletes should be given an outlet to express concerns of uneven power dynamics with someone who can actually make a difference. In the current study, athletes were found to express their concerns to the athletic trainers; however, these individuals do not have the power to make otherwise advisable changes to lessen the degree of biographical disruption that injured athletes' experience.

## Limitations

This study has various limitations that I outline next. One major limitation of this study is the lack of class analysis since data were not collected on social class. Social class is a major factor in the healthcare system and may influence how athletes mobilize resources for injuries. Future research should examine whether explanations concerning etiology and the recommendations for treatment of injury differ by varying social locations such as social class.

Another limitation of this study is that coaches were not interviewed to understand their role in the injury experience (Newman and Weiss 2018). While interviews with sports medicine staff and athletes allowed insight into the coach-athlete and coach–sports medicine staff relationship, the coaches' roles vary. For example, sports medicine staff noted that coaches differed in their level of involvement surrounding injury. Some coaches gave all the power to the sports medicine staff to decide whether an athlete should return to play, while other coaches made the ultimate decision, despite recommendations from the NCAA (2014: 8) that "coaches must not be allowed to impose demands that are inconsistent with guidelines and recommendations established by sports medicine and athletic training professional organizations." While the meaning of health and injury is also influenced by the values and norms of the coaching staff, the current study did not examine this in detail. Therefore, further exploration of the role of coaches in the injury experience is recommended.

## Conclusions

Through observations in the ATC and interviews of both injured collegiate athletes and sports medicine staff members, three main findings are revealed that contribute to understanding health in collegiate athletics. The first, in Chapters 1–4, revealed that organizational issues (i.e., sense-making and the ATC as a contested terrain) take over the care provided to athletes. In turn, these organizational issues result in the objectification of the bodies of both athletes and sports medicine staff. The second finding, in Chapters 5–7, revealed that the ATC operates according to the definitions of gendered and racialized organizations, which affects the meaning of injury for athletes and sports medicine staff members. As with similar organizations, dominant ideologies of gender and race are reinforced through various mechanisms such as stereotyping (Steele and Aronson 1995; Steele 1997), coercion, evasion, exclusion, and silencing. The reinforcement of these dominant ideologies affects the care that athletes receive, which is highlighted by contrasting the care profit-generating sport athletes receive in the ATC with that of non-profit-generating sport athletes. In Chapters 8 and 9, the third main finding revealed is that both acute and chronic injuries result in a biographical disruption; however, the type of biographical disruption differs between the two classes of injuries. Both acute and chronic injuries were recognized as such by athletes when they were unable to use their bodies. However, those with acute injuries did not necessarily experience pain. Different from this position, athletes with chronic injuries often played through pain until they were physically unable to continue.

This book examines how the commodification of the athlete body in the sports-industrial complex is put before the health of the athlete (or caring for athlete health) at an organizational level due to the neoliberal model (as part of which dominant ideologies of race and gender are present, which contrasts with the stated tenets of the athlete healthcare system and sports medicine staff members). This causes more time and attention to be paid to able-bodied profit-generating sport athletes. However, when profit-generating sport athletes are injured beyond repair, the organization's concern for them diminishes. The reality is that the organization has limited resources to help athletes who experience injuries that end their athletic careers because the people that many athletes go to for support (e.g., athletic trainers) are inundated with work helping athletes who are physically "fixable."

Profit-generating sport athletes, and athletes who embody masculinity, are prioritized in the ATC and disproportionately receive its resources and attention. On some level, this strategy makes sense because generating profit is important and pays the bills, thus making the operation of a high-quality ATC possible. However, this practice adversely affects both the non-profit-generating sport athletes and the profit-generating sport athletes who can no longer play. Furthermore, within the ATC, there are dominant ideologies of gender and race. These ideologies make the ATC a hostile space that affects the biography of athletes who experience an injury (e.g., making it less likely for athletes to seek help in the ATC when injured).

Findings from this study reveal that all athletes are exploited in the ATC, while athletes from profit-generating sports are also commodified. This is due to the NCAA being a capitalist enterprise whose goals include generating profit. The goal of the ATC *should* be that athletes are treated holistically. However, given the current structure of the organization of the ATC, such a change is not likely. Both sports medicine staff members and athletes would benefit from changing the organization of the ATC.

# Appendixes

## Appendix 1: Theory and Methods

This study utilizes a phenomenological framework to examine the meaning of injury among collegiate athletes and sports medicine staff members. This phenomenological viewpoint comes from an interpretive paradigm that considers every aspect of social life, including organizations, as fundamentally interpretive. Following the work of the philosopher Maurice Merleau-Ponty (1962), this research is informed by the understanding that the body is an embodied form of consciousness. Merleau-Ponty, a phenomenologist, was interested in the meaning of human experience. Phenomenologists argue that the body needs to be looked at subjectively. To understand phenomenology, this philosophy should be viewed as rejecting Cartesianism. Cartesianism, also known as dualism, has allowed sport scientists to make claims about neutrality and objectivity, specifically through the practice of sports medicine and the biomedical approach. There is an inherent dualistic approach within the ATC that contributes to translating what the philosopher Edmund Husserl (1931) calls the "lived experiences" of athletes into abstract medical knowledge. Using phenomenology, this study shows the strengths of using a nondualistic approach to understand health among collegiate athletes. Opposing Cartesianism, within phenomenology, there is no dualism. The body, therefore, is no longer a thing but an ongoing project that is constructed and experienced.

## Data Collection

Once I received approval for this study by the Institutional Review Board, observations and interviews were conducted. All the observations and a majority of the interviews were conducted in person in the ATC on the NLU campus (except two that were conducted via Zoom). Interviews ranged from thirty to ninety minutes. I explained the purpose of the study before the start of the interview and respondents were asked to provide written consent. Interviews with sports medicine staff were unstructured. Questions about injury and the resources available in the ATC were asked. Examples of the questions include: "How do you understand injury?" "How do you know when an athlete is injured?" "What is the protocol when an athlete is injured?" "What is the purpose of the Athletic Training Center?" "What are the resources available to athletes when they experience an injury?" Interviews with injured athletes were also unstructured. Questions to them focused on the injury experience. Examples of the questions include: "Can you tell me about your first, worst, and current injury?" "Why is that injury your worst?" "How is your current injury different from your first injury?" "What does a typical day of treatment look like in the ATC for you?" "What services do you utilize for social support?"

## Reflexivity

As a trained medical sociologist and race/ethnicity/immigration scholar, I delve more deeply into issues that arise in sport, including those in collegiate sport, specifically focusing on collegiate athlete healthcare. My personal identity impacts the research I conducted. I am a former NCAA Division I athlete who competed at two different universities (transferring to a new university my junior year). I experienced injuries at both universities, which resulted in me spending time in two different ATCs. While I was a Division I NCAA athlete for four years, my experiences also derive from the social location of being a white woman with U.S. citizenship. Therefore, I do not have the same experiences as women athletes of color, men athletes, or athletes who are not U.S. citizens. Additionally, I am not a sports medicine professional, therefore, I do not have the same experiences with this population.

Being a former NCAA Division I athlete biases my findings because I have prior experience in this institutionalized space. However, if I were not a former collegiate athlete, I believe that I would not have been able to develop the same high degree of rapport with sports medicine staff or injured athletes. During observations and interviews, I was often asked by sports medicine staff and athletes if I played a sport in college and/or experienced injuries. Answering yes to both questions, I often saw sports medicine staff and athletes relax and have more of a conversation with me, as opposed to feeling that they were being interviewed.

Identifying as a former collegiate athlete who experienced injuries gave me a certain status that allowed me better access to those in the college sport community. I present as an athlete with my looks, which made me fit in with the community. While conducting observations and interviews in the ATC, I started by wearing the clothes I taught in (i.e., dresses and skirts), and then I eventually ended up bringing athletic clothes to change into so that I would blend in with the sports medicine staff and athletes.

*Contributions to Theory*

This study adds to the theoretical literature by utilizing a phenomenological framework to highlight how power operates in organizations (O'Neill 1972). Through this phenomenological approach, various mechanisms were revealed that are used to enforce the dominant ideologies of masculinity and whiteness, such as stereotyping, coercion, evasion, exclusion, and silencing. For example, sports medicine staff who use their hierarchical relationship to athletes to induce them to perform a behavior (e.g., playing through an injury) exhibit power. This power dynamic was recognized through observations of interactions in the ATC and conversations with sports medicine staff and injured athletes. Power is often discreet, however, utilizing a phenomenological framework allowed for instances of power differentials to be revealed (Foucault [1975] 1977).

In addition, given the limited phenomenological research on athlete bodies by sport sociologists and medical sociologists, the current study adds to the theoretical literature by using a phenomenological framework to further understand institutionalized medicine, how power operates in ATCs, gendered and racialized organizations, and the nuances associated with chronic and acute injuries as forms of biographical disruption.

## Appendix 2: Participant Demographics

Appendix 2 includes the demographics of injured athletes and sports medicine staff members both from interviews and observations that are included in the manuscript.

TABLE A2.1 INJURED ATHLETES DEMOGRAPHICS

| Name | Gender | Race/Ethnicity/Nationality | Sport | Injury Location |
|---|---|---|---|---|
| Alice | Woman | White/domestic | Swimming and diving | Knee |
| Amanda | Woman | White/Latina/domestic | Volleyball | Knee |
| Anthony | Man | Black/domestic | Cross-country/track-and-field | Shoulder |
| Ashley | Woman | White/Hispanic/international | Tennis | Wrist |
| Brianna | Woman | White/domestic | Rowing | Wrist |
| Ben | Man | White/domestic | Swimming and diving | Back |
| Chloe | Woman | White/domestic | Cross-country/track-and-field | Foot |
| Damien | Man | Black/domestic | Track-and-field | Quad |
| Diane | Woman | White/international | Tennis | Wrist |
| Elijah | Man | Black/domestic | Football | Quad |
| Emily | Woman | White/domestic | Basketball | Hip |
| Isabella | Woman | White/Latina/domestic | Soccer | Knee |
| Jackie | Woman | White/Latina/domestic | Soccer | Knee |
| Jack | Man | Black/domestic | Football | Spinal cord |
| Jared | Man | Black/domestic | Football | Ankle |
| Jennifer | Woman | White/international | Swimming and diving | Shoulder |
| Joe | Man | Black/domestic | Track-and-field | Hip |
| Jocelyn | Woman | White/international | Rowing | Shoulder |
| Joni | Woman | White/international | Golf | Spinal cord |
| Josh | Man | White/domestic | Baseball | Shoulder |

| Name | Gender | Race/Origin | Sport | Injury |
|---|---|---|---|---|
| Julian | Man | Black/Latino/domestic | Baseball | Wrist |
| Kate | Woman | White/international | Basketball | Knee |
| Kyle | Man | Indigenous/Latino/domestic | Football | Foot |
| Lily | Woman | White/international | Rowing | Rib |
| Luke | Man | Black/domestic | Football | Knee |
| Maddie | Woman | Black/domestic | Soccer | Knee |
| Matthew | Man | White/domestic | Football | Knee |
| Mark | Man | White/Latino/domestic | Baseball | Knee |
| Mary | Woman | Asian/international | Swimming and diving | Spinal cord |
| Michelle | Woman | Black/domestic | Track-and-field | Head |
| Miles | Man | Black/domestic | Football | Wrist |
| Rachel | Woman | White/domestic | Cross-country/track-and-field | Foot |
| Ray | Man | Black/domestic | Cross-country/track-and-field | Achilles |
| Sam | Man | White/international | Tennis | Spinal cord |
| Sophie | Woman | White/international | Rowing | Shoulder |
| Tasha | Woman | White/international | Rowing | Shoulder |
| Tanner | Man | White/Latino/domestic | Baseball | Shoulder |
| Taylor | Woman | Black/domestic | Track-and-field | Wrist |
| Terrence | Man | White/domestic | Football | Knee |
| Tim | Man | Black/international | Basketball | Knee |
| Tyson | Man | Black/domestic | Track-and-field | Quad |
| Zach | Man | White/domestic | Baseball | Shoulder |

## TABLE A2.2 SPORTS MEDICINE STAFF DEMOGRAPHICS

| Name | Gender | Race/Ethnicity/Nationality | Sport | Position |
|---|---|---|---|---|
| Alex | Man | White/domestic | Football | Undergraduate athletic training student |
| Anne | Woman | White/Latina/domestic | All sports | Physical therapist/athletic trainer |
| Brian | Man | White/domestic | Football | Athletic trainer |
| Catherine | Woman | White/domestic | All sports | Physician |
| Charles | Man | Black/international | All sports | Physician |
| David | Man | Black/domestic | Soccer | Athletic trainer |
| Derek | Man | White/domestic | Football | Athletic trainer |
| Elizabeth | Woman | White/domestic | All sports | Doctor of physical therapy student |
| George | Man | White/domestic | All sports | Sport psychologist |
| James | Man | White/domestic | Baseball | Athletic trainer |
| Jane | Woman | White/domestic | All sports | Nutritionist |
| Joe | Man | Asian/domestic | Cross-country/rowing | Athletic trainer |
| John | Man | White/Latino/domestic | All sports | Physical therapist |
| Justine | Woman | Black/domestic | Football | Undergraduate athletic training student |
| Katie | Woman | White/domestic | Track-and-field | Athletic trainer |
| Maria | Woman | White/domestic | Cross-country/track-and-field | Athletic trainer |
| Michael | Man | White/Latino/domestic | Baseball + all sports | Physical therapist |
| Nancy | Woman | White/domestic | Tennis | Athletic trainer |
| Noah | Man | White/domestic | Football + all sports | Athletic trainer |
| Oliver | Man | White/domestic | Football | Athletic trainer |
| Rick | Man | White/domestic | All sports | Doctor of physical therapy student |
| Sammy | Woman | Black/domestic | Football | Undergraduate athletic training student |
| Tom | Man | White/Latino/domestic | All sports | Physical therapist |
| William | Man | White/domestic | All sports | Physician |

# References

Acker, Joan. 1990. "Hierarchies, Jobs, Bodies: A Theory of Gendered Organizations." *Gender and Society* 4 (2): 139–158.

Adler, Patricia, and Peter Adler. 1991. *Backboards and Blackboards: College Athletes and Role Engulfment*. New York: Columbia University Press.

Allen-Collinson, Jacquelyn, and John Hockey. 2007. "'Working Out' Identity: Distance Runners and the Management of Disrupted Identity." *Leisure Studies* 26 (4): 381–398.

Allison, Rachel. 2018. *Kicking Center: Gender and the Selling of Women's Professional Soccer*. New Brunswick, NJ: Rutgers University Press.

American College of Sports Medicine (ACSM). 2023. "About Us." Accessed May 8, 2023. Available at https://www.acsm.org/about.

Anderson, Elijah. 2015. "The White Space." *Sociology of Race and Ethnicity* 1 (1): 10–21.

Balint, Enid. 1969. "The Possibilities of Patient-Centered Medicine." *Journal of the Royal College of General Practitioners* 17 (82): 269–276.

Barbour, Allen B. 1995. *Caring for Patients: A Critique of the Medical Model*. Stanford, CA: Stanford University Press.

Bass, Jordon, Clair Schaeperkoetter, and Kyle Bunds. 2015. "The 'Front Porch': Examining the Increasing Interconnection of University and Athletic Department Funding." *ASHE Higher Education Report* 41(5).

Beauvoir, Simone de. 1949. *The Second Sex*. Translated by Constance Borde and Sheila Malovany-Chevallier. New York: Vintage Books.

Bell, Derrick. 1993. *Faces at the Bottom of the Well: The Permanence of Racism.* New York: Basic Books.
Berger, Peter, and Thomas Luckmann. 1966. *The Social Construction of Reality: A Treatise on the Sociology of Knowledge.* New York: Anchor Books.
Berryman, Jack W. 1995. *Out of Many, One: A History of the American College of Sports Medicine.* Champaign, IL: Human Kinetics.
Bimper, Albert, Jr. 2020. *Black Collegiate Athletes and the Neoliberal State: Dreaming from Bended Knee.* Lanham, MD: Rowman and Littlefield.
Bittner, Egon. 1990. *Aspects of Police Work.* Boston: Northeastern University Press.
Blumer, Herbert. 1958. "Race Prejudice as a Sense of Group Position." *Pacific Sociological Review* 1 (1): 3–7.
Bonilla-Silva, Eduardo. 2001. *White Supremacy and Racism in the Post–Civil Rights Era.* Boulder, CO: Lynne Rienner.
Bourdieu, Pierre. (1984) 2012. *Distinction: A Social Critique of the Judgement of Taste.* Translated by Richard Nice. London: Routledge.
Brewer, Britton W., and Albert J. Petitpas. 2017. "Athletic Identity Foreclosure." *Current Opinion in Psychology* 16:118–122.
Brewer, Britton W., Judy L. Van Raalte, and Darwyn E. Linder. 1993. "Athletic Identity: Hercules' Muscles or Achilles Heel?" *International Journal of Sport Psychology* 24 (2): 237–254.
Brohm, Jean-Marie. 1978. *Sport—A Prison of Measured Time: Essays by Jean-Marie Brohm.* London: Ink Links.
Burrell, Gibson. 1997. *Pandemonium: Towards a Retro-Organization Theory.* London: Sage.
Bury, Michael. 1982. "Chronic Illness as Biographical Disruption." *Sociology of Health and Illness* 4 (2): 1–17.
Butler, Judith. 1988. "Performative Acts and Gender Constitution: An Essay in Phenomenology and Feminist Theory." *Theatre Journal* 40 (4): 519–531.
Byers, Walter, and Charles Hammer. 1995. *Unsportsmanlike Conduct: Exploiting College Athletes.* Ann Arbor: University of Michigan Press.
Canada, Tracie, Kaitlin Pericak, and Miray D. Seward. 2022. "Amateurism as a Narrative of Control: An Interdisciplinary Approach to the Lived Experiences of College Athletes." *Sports Innovation Journal* SI:55–68.
Carricaburu, Danièle, and Janine Pierret. 1995. "From Biographical Disruption to Biographical Reinforcement: The Case of HIV-Positive Men." *Sociology of Health and Illness* 17 (1): 65–88.
Carrington, Ben. 2010. *Sport, Race, and Politics: The Sporting Black Diaspora.* London: Sage.
Carter-Francique, Akilah R., and Courtney L. Flowers. 2013. "Intersections of Race, Ethnicity, and Gender in Sport." In *Gender Relations in Sport*, edited by Emily A. Roper, 73–93. Rotterdam, NL: Sense.
Chambat, Pierre, Christian Guier, Bertrand Sonnery-Cottet, Jean-Marie Fayard, and Mathieu Thaunat. 2013. "The Evolution of ACL Reconstruction over the Last Fifty Years." *International Orthopaedics* 37 (2): 181–186.

Coakley, Jay. 2015. "Assessing the Sociology of Sport: On Cultural Sensibilities and the Great Sport Myth." *International Review for the Sociology of Sport* 50 (4–5): 402–406.
Comeaux, Eddie. 2017. *College Athletes' Rights and Well-Being: Critical Perspectives on Policy and Practice.* Baltimore: Johns Hopkins University Press.
Commission on Accreditation of Athletic Training Education (CAATE). 2023. "Who We Are." Accessed May 8, 2023. Available at https://caate.net/About-CAATE/Who-We-Are.
Connell, Raewyn W. 1987. *Gender and Power: Society, the Person, and Sexual Politics.* Cambridge: Blackwell.
———. 1997. "Gender Politics for Men." *International Journal of Sociology and Social Policy* 17 (1–2): 62–77.
Cooky, Cheryl, Michael Messner, and Michela Musto. 2015. "'It's Dude Time!': A Quarter Century of Excluding Women's Sports in Televised News and Highlight Shows." *Communication and Sport* 3 (3): 261–287.
Cooper, Joseph N., Akuoma Nwadike, and Charles Macaulay. 2017. "A Critical Race Theory Analysis of Big-Time College Sports: Implications for Culturally Responsive and Race-Conscious Sport Leadership." *Journal of Issues in Intercollegiate Athletics* 10:204–233.
Cottom, Tressie McMillan. 2019. *Thick: And Other Essays.* New York: New Press.
Courson, Ron, Michael Goldenberg, Kevin Adams, Scott Anderson, Bob Colgate, Larry Cooper, Lori Dewald, R. T. Floyd, Douglas Gregory, Peter Indelicato, David Klossner, Rick O'Leary, Tracy Ray, Tim Selgo, Charlie Thompson, and Gary Turbak. 2014. "Inter-Association Consensus Statement on Best Practices for Sports Medicine Management for Secondary Schools and College." *Journal of Athletic Training* 49 (1): 128–137.
Crawford, Robert. 2006. "Health as a Meaningful Social Practice." *Health: An Interdisciplinary Journal for the Social Study of Health, Illness and Medicine* 10 (4): 401–420.
Crenshaw, Kimberlé. 1989. "Demarginalizing the Intersection of Race and Sex: A Black Feminist Critique of Antidiscrimination Doctrine, Feminist Theory and Antiracist Politics." *University of Chicago Legal Forum* 1 (8): 139–167.
Creswell, John, and Cheryl Poth. 2007. *Qualitative Inquiry and Research Design: Choosing among Five Approaches.* Thousand Oaks, CA: Sage.
Curry, Timothy Jon. 1993. "A Little Pain Never Hurt Anyone: Athletic Career Socialization and the Normalization of Sports Injury." *Symbolic Interaction* 16 (3): 273–290.
Davis, Lennard J. 2010. "Constructing Normalcy." In *The Disability Studies Reader*, 3rd ed., edited by Lennard J. Davis, 3–19. New York: Routledge.
Delgado, Richard, and Jean Stefancic. 2017. *Critical Race Theory: An Introduction.* 3rd ed. New York: New York University Press.
Desmond, Matthew, and Mustafa Emirbayer. 2020. *Race in America.* 2nd ed. New York: W. W. Norton.

Dixon, Nicholas. 2021. "Sport, Meritocracy, and Praise." *Journal of the Philosophy of Sport* 48 (2): 275–292.
Dubal, Sam. 2010. "The Neoliberalization of Football: Rethinking Neoliberalism through Commercialization of the Beautiful Game." *International Review for the Sociology of Sport* 45 (2): 123–146.
Du Bois, W.E.B. (1903) 1989. *The Souls of Black Folk*. New York: Penguin Books.
Dunbar-Ortiz, Roxanne. 2014. *An Indigenous Peoples' History of the United States*. Boston: Beacon.
Eckstein, Rick. 2017. *How College Athletics Are Hurting Girls' Sports: The Pay to Play Pipeline*. Lanham, MD: Rowman and Littlefield.
Edwards, Harry. 1969. *The Revolt of the Black Athlete*. New York: Free Press.
———. 1973. *Sociology of Sport*. Homewood, IL: Dorsey.
———. 1984. "The Black 'Dumb Jock': An American Sports Tragedy." *College Board Review* 131:8–13.
Edwards, Richard. 1979. *Contested Terrain: The Transformation of the Workplace in the Twentieth Century*. New York: Basic Books.
Eitzen, D. Stanley. 2009. *Fair and Foul: Beyond the Myths and Paradoxes of Sport*. 4th ed. Lanham, MA: Rowman and Littlefield.
Engel, George L. 1977. "The Need for a New Medical Model: A Challenge for Biomedicine." *Science* 196 (4286): 129–136.
Feagin, Joe. 2006. *Systemic Racism: A Theory of Oppression*. New York: Routledge.
Ferguson, Tomika, and James W. Satterfield. 2016. "Black Women Athletes and the Performance of Hyper-Femininity." In *Critical Perspectives on Black Women and College Success*, edited by Lori D. Patton and Natasha N. Croom, 115–126. New York: Routledge.
Fleming, Crystal M. 2018. *How to Be Less Stupid about Race: On Racism, White Supremacy, and the Racial Divide*. Boston: Beacon.
Flowers, Courtney, Jasmine Hamilton, and Joyce Olushola Ogunrinde. 2023. "Examining the Ability of Title IX to Provide Equitable Participation Opportunities for Black Women College Athletes." *Journal of Intercollegiate Sport* 16 (1): 6–24.
Foucault, Michel. (1963) 1973. *The Birth of the Clinic: An Archaeology of Medical Perception*. Translated by Alan Sheridan. New York: Pantheon.
———. (1975) 1977. *Discipline and Punish: The Birth of the Prison*. Translated by Alan Sheridan. New York: Vintage.
Freidson, Eliot. 1970. *Profession of Medicine: A Study of the Sociology of Applied Knowledge*. New York: Dodd, Mead.
Frey, James H. 1991. "Social Risk and the Meaning of Sport." *Sociology of Sport Journal* 8:136–145.
Frey, James H., and Stanley D. Eitzen. 1991. "Sport and Society." *Annual Review of Sociology* 17:503–522.
Friedland, Roger, and Robert Alford. 1991. "Bringing Society Back In: Symbols, Practices, and Institutional Contradictions." In *The New Institutionalism in*

*Organizational Analysis*, edited by W. W. Powell and P. J. DiMaggio, 232–267. Chicago: University of Chicago Press.
Gadamer, Hans-Georg. 1996. *The Enigma of Health: The Art of Healing in a Scientific Age*. Translated by Jason Gaiger and Nicholas Walker. Stanford, CA: Stanford University Press.
Gaston Gayles, Joy, Eddie Comeaux, Ezinne Ofoegbu, and Sara Grummert. 2018. "Neoliberal Capitalism and Racism in College Athletics: Critical Approaches for Supporting Student-Athletes." *New Directions for Student Services* 163:11–21.
Giardina, Michael D., and Joshua I. Newman. 2014. "The Politics of Research." In *The Oxford Handbook of Qualitative Research*, edited by Patricia Leavy, 699–723. New York: Oxford University Press.
Gilmore, Ruth Wilson. 2017. "Abolition Geography and the Problem of Innocence." In *Futures of Black Radicalism*, edited by Gaye Theresa Johnson and Alex Lubin, 55–77. London: Verso.
Goffman, Erving. 1961. *Asylums: Essays on the Social Situations of Mental Patients and Other Inmates*. New York: Doubleday.
———. 1963. *Stigma: Notes on the Management of Spoiled Identity*. New York: Simon and Schuster.
Gorse, Keith, Francis Feld, and Robert Blanc. 2017. *True Stories from the Athletic Training Room*. West Deptford, NJ: Slack.
Gramsci, Antonio. 1995. *Further Selections from the Prison Notebooks*. Translated by Derek Boothman. London: Lawrence and Wishart.
Hall, Ann. 1985. "How Should We Theorize Sport in a Capitalist Patriarchy?" *International Review for the Sociology of Sport* 20 (1–2): 109–115.
Hartmann, Douglas. 2001. "Sport as Contested Terrain." In *Companion to Racial and Ethnic Studies*, edited by John Solomos and David Theo Goldberg, 405–415. Hoboken, NJ: Blackwell.
Harvey, David. 2005. *A Brief History of Neoliberalism*. Oxford: Oxford University Press.
Hasbrook, Cythina A., and Othello Harris. 2000. "Wrestling with Gender: Physicality and Masculinities among Inner-City First and Second Graders." In *Masculinities, Gender Relations, and Sport*, edited by Jim McKay, Michael A. Messner, and Don Sabo, 13–30. Thousand Oaks, CA: Sage.
Haslerig, Siduri, Rican Vue, and Sara Grummert. 2020. "Invincible Bodies: American Sport Media's Racialization of Black and White College Football Players." *International Review for the Sociology of Sport* 55 (3): 272–290.
Hatteberg, Sarah. 2018. "Under Surveillance: Collegiate Athletics as a Total Institution." *Sociology of Sport Journal* 35:149–158.
Hawkins, Billy. 2010. *The New Plantation: Black Athletes, College Sports, and Predominantly White NCAA Institutions*. New York: Palgrave MacMillan.
Hearn, Jeff, and P. Wendy Parkin. 1987. *Sex at Work*. Brighton: Wheatsheaf.
Heller, Henry. 2016. *The Capitalist University: The Transformations of Higher Education in the United States since 1945*. London: Pluto Press.

Hextrum, Kirsten. 2020a. "Amateurism Revisited: How U.S. College Athletic Recruitment Favors Middle-Class Athletes." *Sport, Education and Society* 25 (1): 111–123.

———. 2020b. "Bigger, Faster, Stronger: How Racist and Sexist Ideologies Persist in College Sports." *Gender and Education* 32 (8): 1053–1071.

———. 2021. *Special Admission: How College Sports Recruitment Favors White Suburban Athletes*. New Brunswick, NJ: Rutgers University Press.

Hextrum, Kirsten, and Simran Sethi. 2021. "Title IX at 50: Legitimating State Domination of Women's Sport." *International Review for the Sociology of Sport* 57 (5): 655–672.

Hoberman, John. 1944. *Mortal Engines: The Science of Performance and the Dehumanization of Sport*. Caldwell, NJ: Blackburn.

Hoffman, Jennifer Lee. 2020. *College Sports and Institutional Values in Competition: Leadership Challenges*. New York: Routledge.

Hogarth, Rana A. 2017. *Medicalizing Blackness: Making Racial Difference in the Atlantic World, 1780–1940*. Chapel Hill: University of North Carolina Press.

Hughes, Robert, and Jay Coakley. 1991. "Positive Deviance among Athletes: The Implications of Overconformity to the Sport Ethic." *Sociology of Sport Journal* 8:307–325.

Hums, Mary, and Joanne MacLean. 2004. *Governance and Policy in Sport Organizations*. Scottsdale, AZ: Hathaway.

Husserl, Edmund. 1931. *Cartesian Meditations: An Introduction to Phenomenology*. Translated by Dorion Cairns. Amsterdam, NL: Kluwer Academic Publishers.

Ibrahim, Hilmi. 1975. *Sport and Society: An Introduction to Sociology of Sport*. Long Beach, CA: Hwong.

Kalman-Lamb, Nathan. 2018. *Game Misconduct: Injury, Fandom, and the Business of Sport*. Nova Scotia, Canada: Fernwood.

———. 2019. "Athletic Labor and Social Reproduction." *Journal of Sport and Social Issues* 43 (6): 515–530.

Kanter, Rosabeth Moss. 1977. *Men and Women of the Corporation*. New York: Basic Books.

Keaton, Ajhanai C. I. 2021. "A Critical Discourse Analysis of Racial Narratives from White Athletes Attending a Historically Black College/University." *Qualitative Research in Sport, Exercise, and Health* 6:1–18.

———. 2022. "Black Women Diversity Leaders' Perceptions of Organizational Inclusivity in College Sports." *Frontiers in Sports and Active Living* 4 (923649): 1–13.

Keaton, Ajhanai C. I., and Joseph N. Cooper. 2022. "A Racial Reckoning in Racialized Organizations? Applying Racialized Organization Theory to the NCAA Institutional Field." *Journal of Issues in Intercollegiate Athletics* 15: 189–218.

Kidd, Victor, Richard Southall, Mark Nagel, Jerry Reynolds, Anna Scheyett, and Christian Anderson. 2018. "Profit Athletes' Athletic Role Set and Post-Athletic Transitions." *Journal of Issues in Intercollegiate Athletics* 11:115–141.

King, Samantha. 2012. "Nike U: Full-Program Athletics Contracts and the Corporate University." In *Sport and Neoliberalism: Politics, Consumption, and Culture*, edited by David L. Andrews and Michael L. Silk, 75–89. Philadelphia: Temple University Press.
King-White, Ryan. 2018. *Sport and the Neoliberal University: Profit, Politics, and Pedagogy*. New Brunswick, NJ: Rutgers University Press.
Koch, James. 1973. A Troubled Cartel: The NCAA. *Law and Contemporary Problems* 38 (1): 135–150.
Lindblom, Charles. 1959. "The Science of 'Muddling Through.'" *Public Administration Review* 19 (2): 79–88.
Link, Bruce, and Jo Phelan. 1995. "Social Conditions as Fundamental Causes of Disease." *Journal of Health and Social Behavior* (extra issue): 80–94.
Lopez, Ian Haney. 1996. *White by Law: The Legal Construction of Race*. New York: New York University Press.
Luhmann, Niklas. 1979. *Trust and Power*. Translated by Howard Davis, John Raffan, and Kathryn Rooney. Cambridge: Polity.
Lune, Howard. 2010. *Understanding Organizations*. Cambridge: Polity.
Mackie, Jim. 2019. *Just Another Smelly Foot: The History of Athletic Training and Gatorade at the University of Florida*. Self-published.
Maguire, Joseph. 2005. *Power and Global Sport: Zones of Prestige, Emulation, and Resistance*. London: Routledge.
Malcolm, Dominic, and Emma Pullen. 2018. "'Everything I Enjoy Doing I Just Couldn't Do': Biographical Disruption for Sport-Related Injury." *Health* 24 (4): 366–383.
Marmot, Michael. 2005. "Social Determinants of Health Inequalities." *Lancet* 365:1099–1104.
Marx, Karl. 1844. *Economic and Philosophical Manuscripts of 1844*. Translated by Edward Shils and Max Rheinstein. Cambridge, MA: Harvard University Press.
———. 1867. *Das Kapital: A Critique of Political Economy*. Translated by Samuel Moore. Seattle, WA: Pacific Publishing.
McRuer, Robert. 2006. *Crip Theory: Cultural Signs of Queerness and Disability*. New York: New York University Press.
Melamed, Jodi. 2015. "Racial Capitalism." *Critical Ethnic Studies* 1 (1): 76–85.
Merleau-Ponty, Maurice. 1962. *Phenomenology of Perception*. Translated by Colin Smith. London, UK: Routledge.
Messner, Michael. 1992. *Power at Play: Sports and the Problem of Masculinity*. Boston: Beacon.
Morden, Andrew, Clare Jinks, and Bie Nio Ong. 2015. "Risk and Self-Managing Chronic Joint Pain: Looking beyond Individual Lifestyles and Behaviour." *Sociology of Health and Illness* 37 (6): 888–903.
Mulvey, Laura. 1975. "Visual Pleasure and Narrative Cinema." *Screen* 16 (3): 6–18.
National Athletic Trainers' Association (NATA). 2021. "Athletic Training." Accessed May 8, 2023. Available at https://www.nata.org/about/athletic-training.

National Center for Education Statistics (NCES). 2019. "Back-to-School Statistics." Accessed September 5, 2019. Available at https://nces.ed.gov/fastfacts/display.asp?id=372#College_enrollment.

National Collegiate Athletic Association (NCAA). 2014. *2014–2015 NCAA Sports Medicine Handbook*. Indianapolis, IN: National Collegiate Athletic Association.

———. 2017. *Athletics Healthcare Administrator Handbook: A Guide for Designated Athletics Healthcare Administrators*. Accessed May 29, 2024. Available at https://ncaaorg.s3.amazonaws.com/ssi/ahca/SSI_AHCAHandbook.pdf.

———. 2019a. "Division I Student-Athlete Advisory Committees." Accessed May 21, 2019. Available at https://www.ncaa.org/sports/2013/11/18/division-i-student-athlete-advisory-committee.aspx.

———. 2019b. "Student-Athletes." Accessed September 5, 2019. Available at http://www.ncaa.org/student-athletes.

———. 2020. "What Is the NCAA?" Accessed August 19, 2020. Available at http://www.ncaa.org/about/resources/media-center/ncaa-101/what-ncaa.

———. 2021a. "Athletics Health Care Administration Best Practices: Independent Medical Care for College Student-Athlete Guidelines." Accessed February 6, 2021. Available at https://www.ncaa.org/sport-science-institute/athletics-health-care-administration-best-practices-0.

———. 2021b. "Loss-of-Value Insurance White Paper." Accessed February 6, 2021. Available at https://www.ncaa.org/about/resources/insurance/loss-value-insurance-White-paper.

———. 2022. "History." Accessed March 21, 2022. Available at https://www.ncaa.org/sports/2021/5/4/history.aspx.

———. 2023a. *Division I 2023–2024 Manual*. Accessed January 6, 2024. Available at https://www.ncaapublications.com/productdownloads/D124.pdf.

———. 2023b. "Finances." Accessed July 11, 2023. Available at https://www.ncaa.org/sports/2021/5/4/finances.aspx.

———. 2023c. "NCAA Student-Athlete Medical Insurance Legislation." Accessed May 8, 2023. Available at https://www.ncaa.org/sports/2013/11/22/ncaa-student-athlete-medical-insurance-legislation.aspx.

———. 2024a. "Mission and Priorities." Accessed January 15, 2024. Available at https://www.ncaa.org/sports/2021/6/28/mission-and-priorities.aspx.

———. 2024b. "NCAA Demographics Database." Accessed May 28, 2024. Available at https://www.ncaa.org/sports/2018/12/13/ncaa-demographics-database.aspx.

———. 2024c. "Overview." Accessed January 5, 2024. Available at https://www.ncaa.org/sports/2021/2/16/overview.aspx.

Newcomer, Kathryn E., Harry P. Hatry, and Joseph S. Wholey. 2015. *Handbook of Practical Program Evaluation*. 4th ed. Hoboken, NJ: Wiley.

Newell, Emily M., and Simran Kaur Sethi. 2023. "Exploring the Perception of Division I Coaches and Administrators about International Collegiate Athlete Exclusion from Name, Image, and Likeness Opportunities." *Journal of Sport Management* 37 (5): 345–358.

Newman, Nathan D., and Windee M. Weiss. 2018. "Relationship between Demographic Variables and Collegiate Athletes' Perceptions of Social Support from Head Coaches." *International Journal of Sports Science and Coaching* 13 (3): 343–348.

Nixon, Howard, II. 1993. "Accepting Risks of Pain and Injury in Sport: Mediated Cultural Influences on Playing Hurt." *Sociology of Sport Journal* 10:183–196.

———. 1994. "Coaches' Views of Risk, Pain, and Injury in Sport, with Special Reference to Gender Differences." *Sociology of Sport Journal* 11:79–87.

Ofoegbu, Ezinne, and Leslie Ekpe. 2022. "Walk It Like You Talk It: A Critical Discourse Analysis of College Athletics Response to the Murder of George Floyd." *Journal of Issues in Intercollegiate Athletics* 15:168–188.

Oluo, Ijeoma. 2018. *So You Want to Talk about Race.* New York: Seal.

Omi, Michael, and Howard Winant. 2015. *Racial Formation in the United States.* 3rd ed. New York: Routledge.

O'Neill, John. 1972. "Can Phenomenology be Critical?" *Philosophy of the Social Sciences* 2:1–13.

Pena-López, José Atilano, and José Manuel Sánchez-Santos. 2017. "Individual Social Capital: Accessibility and Mobilization of Resources Embedded in Social Networks." *Social Networks* 49 (2): 1–11.

Pericak, Kaitlin, and Caitlin Vitosky Clarke. 2023. "Embodied Regulation: The Case of Women Collegiate Athletes." *Sport in Society* 26 (12): 1957–1978.

Perrow, Charles. 1972. *Complex Organizations: A Critical Essay.* Glenview, IL: Scott, Foresman.

President and Fellows of Harvard College. 2023. "A Timeline of Harvard's History." Accessed September 15, 2023. Available at https://www.harvard.edu/about/history/timeline/.

Rapp, Geoffrey Christopher, and Christopher D. Ingersoll. 2019. "Sports Medicine Delivery Models: Legal Risks." *Journal of Athletic Training* 54 (12): 1237–1240.

Ray, Victor. 2019. "A Theory of Racialized Organizations." *American Sociological Review* 84 (1): 26–53.

Rhoden, William. 2006. *Forty Million Dollar Slaves: The Rise, Fall, and Redemption of the Black Athlete.* New York: Three Rivers.

Robinson, Cedric J. 1983. *Black Marxism: The Making of the Black Radical Tradition.* Chapel Hill: University of North Carolina Press.

Rodney, Walter. 1972. *How Europe Underdeveloped Africa.* Washington, DC: Howard University Press.

Sabo, Don. 2009. "Sports Injury, the Pain Principle, and the Promise of Reform." *Journal of Intercollegiate Sports* 2:145–152.

Sack, Allen, and Ellen Staurowsky. 1998. *College Athletes for Hire: The Evolution and Legacy of the NCAA's Amateur Myth.* Westport, CT: Greenwood Publishing Group.

Sage, George, D. Stanley Eitzen, and Becky Beal. 2019. *Sociology of North American Sport.* 11th ed. New York: Oxford University Press.

Sartre, Jean-Paul. 1948. *Anti-Semite and Jew: An Explanation of the Etiology of Hate.* Translated by George J. Becker. New York: Schocken.

———. 1956. *Being and Nothingness.* New York: Philosophical Library.

Schutz, Alfred. 1970. *On Phenomenology and Social Relations.* Chicago: University of Chicago Press.

Scott, W. Richard. 1992. *Organizations: Rational, Natural, and Open Systems.* Englewood Cliffs, NJ: Prentice Hall.

Short, James F. 1984. "The Social Fabric at Risk: Toward the Social Transformation of Risk Analysis." *American Sociological Review* 49:711–725.

Shropshire, Kenneth, and Collin Williams. 2017. *The Miseducation of the Student Athlete: How to Fix College Sports.* Philadelphia: Warton Digital.

Shulman, James, and William Bowen. 2001. *The Game of Life: College Sports and Educational Values.* Princeton, NJ: Princeton University Press.

Silverman, David. 1971. *The Theory of Organisations: A Sociological Framework.* New York: Basic Books.

Simien, Evelyn M., Nneka Arinze, and Jennifer McGarry. 2019. "A Portrait of Marginality in Sport and Education: Toward a Theory of Intersectionality and Raced-Gendered Experiences for Black Female College Athletes." *Journal of Women, Politics and Policy* 40 (3): 409–427.

Singer, John. 2009. "African American Football Athletes' Perspectives on Institutional Integrity in College Sport." *Research Quarterly for Exercise and Sport* 80 (1): 102–116.

Smedley, Brian D., Adrienne Y. Stith, and Alan R. Nelson. 2003. *Unequal Treatment: Confronting Racial and Ethnic Disparities in Health Care.* Washington, DC: National Academies Press.

Southall, Richard M. 2023. "The Exploitation of the Power Five Profit-Athletes." In *The NCAA and the Exploitation of College Profit-Athletes: An Amateurism That Never Was,* edited by Richard M. Southall, Mark S. Nagel, Ellen J. Staurowsky, Richard T. Karcher, and Joel G. Maxcy, 261–289. Columbia: University of South Carolina Press.

Southall, Richard, E. Woodrow Eckard, Mark S. Nagel, and Morgan H. Randall. 2015. "Athletic Success and NCAA Profit-Athletes' Adjusted Graduation Gaps." *Sociology of Sport Journal* 32:395–414.

Southall, Richard, Crystal Southall, and Brendan Dwyer. 2009. "2009 Bowl Championship Series Telecasts: Expressions of Big-Time College-Sport's Commercial Institutional Logics." *Journal of Issues in Intercollegiate Athletics* 2: 150–176.

Southall, Richard M., and Jonathan D. Weiler. 2014. "NCAA Division-I Athletic Departments: 21st Century Athletic Company Towns." *Journal of Issues in Intercollegiate Athletics* 7:161–186.

Starr, Paul. 1982. *The Social Transformation of American Medicine.* New York: Basic Books.

Staurowsky, Ellen, and Alan Sack. 2005. "Reconsidering the Use of the Term Student-Athlete in Academic Research." *Journal of Sport Management* 19 (2): 103–116.

Steele, Claude. 1997. "A Threat in the Air: How Stereotypes Shape Intellectual Identity and Performance." *American Psychologist* 52 (6): 613–629.

Steele, Claude, and Joshua Aronson. 1995. "Stereotype Threat and the Intellectual Test Performance of African Americans." *Journal of Personality and Social Psychology* 69 (5): 797–811.

Sumner, William Graham. 1906. *Folkways*. Boston: Athenaeum.

Theune, Felecia. 2019. "Brown, Title IX and the Impact of Race and Sex Segregation on Sports Participation Opportunities for Black Females." *Sociology Compass* 13 (1): e12661.

Toombs, S. Kay. 1992. *The Meaning of Illness: A Phenomenological Account of the Different Perspectives of Physician and Patient*. Dordrecht, NL: Kluwer Academic.

Turner, Bryan, and Steven Wainwright. 2003. "Corps de Ballet: The Case of the Injured Ballet Dancer." *Sociology of Health and Illness* 25 (4): 269–288.

Turner, Robert. 2018. *Not for Long: The Life and Career of the NFL Athlete*. New York: Oxford University Press.

Twin, Stephanie. 1979. *Out of the Bleachers: Writings on Women and Sport*. Old Westbury, NY: Feminist.

U.S. Census. 2020. "Census Regions and Divisions of the United States." Accessed June 1, 2020. Available at https://www2.census.gov/geo/pdfs/maps-data/maps/reference/us_regdiv.pdf.

U.S. Department of Education. 2021. "Title IX and Sex Discrimination." Accessed May 28, 2024. Available at https://www2.ed.gov/about/offices/list/ocr/docs/tix_dis.html.

Vadeboncoeur, Joshua, and Trevor Bopp. 2020. "[Self]perceptions of Whiteness: An Interpretative Phenomenological Analysis of White College Athletes." *Journal of Issues in Intercollegiate Athletics* 13:119–142.

Valdés, Juan Gabriel. 1995. *Pinochet's Economists: The Chicago School of Economics in Chile*. Cambridge, MA: Cambridge University Press.

Wachs, Faye Linda. 2023. *Metamorphosis: Who We Become after Facial Paralysis*. New Brunswick, NJ: Rutgers University Press.

Walk, Stephan. 2004. "Athletic Trainers: Between Care and Social Control." In *Sporting Bodies, Damaged Selves: Sociological Studies of Sports-Related Injury*, edited by Kevin Young, 251–267. Bingley: Emerald Group.

Ware, Susan. 2007. *Title IX: A Brief History with Documents*. Long Grove, IL: Waveland.

Washburn, Jennifer. 2006. *University, Inc.: The Corporate Corruption of Higher Education*. New York: Basic Books.

Washington, Harriet. 2006. *Medical Apartheid: The Dark History of Medical Experimentation on Black Americans from Colonial Times to the Present*. New York: Doubleday.

Webber, Matt J. 2013. *Dropping the Bucket and Sponge: A History of Early Athletic Training, 1881–1947.* Prescott, AZ: Athletic Training History.
Weber, Max. (1904) 1958. *The Protestant Ethic and Spirit of Capitalism.* Translated by Talcott Parsons. New York: Scribner.
———. (1921) 1978. *Economy and Society: An Outline of Interpretive Sociology.* Edited by Guenther Roth and Claus Wittich. Berkeley: University of California Press.
Weick, Karl. 2001. *Making Sense of the Organization.* Oxford: Blackwell.
West, Candace, and Don Zimmerman. 1987. "Doing Gender." *Gender and Society* 1 (2): 125–151.
Wheeler, Stanton. 2004. "Rethinking Amateurism and the NCAA." *Stanford Law and Policy Review* 15 (1): 213–235.
Zinn, Howard. 1980. *A People's History of the United States.* New York: Harper Collins.
Zirin, Dave. 2011. *Game Over: How Politics Turned the Sports World Upside Down.* New York: New Press.

# Index

Able-bodied, 3, 31, 51, 89, 102, 108, 120
Amateurism, 8–9
American College of Sports Medicine (ACSM), 22, 117
Athlete-centered, 2–3
Athletic Training Center (ATC), 2, 15–16, 30
Athletic training room, 1, 17, 22, 30, 33, 36, 84; Baseball athletic training room, 30, 50, 66; Basketball athletic training room, 30; Main athletic training room, 29–35, 32f, 43, 45, 50–51, 60, 62, 64–66, 68, 70, 74, 77, 84, 89, 113
Autonomy, 7, 24, 109–111, 116

Biographical disruption, 89–92, 114, 119–120; mobilization of resources, 103–112; recognition, 92–96; uncertainty, 97–102

Capital, 4, 11–13, 49
Capitalism, 5, 10–11; free market, 4–5, 9; neoliberal capitalism, 9, 27, 89; racial capitalism, 5–6, 10, 13, 19, 74

Commodity, 5, 9, 12–13, 19, 54, 69, 115, 120–121
Communication, 25, 36, 44, 52, 54–56, 58, 99
Contested terrain, 18–19, 40, 59–61, 119
Critical Race Theory (CRT), 12, 75, 80

Deregulation, 4, 24, 26, 110. *See also* neoliberal
Discrimination, 10, 13, 63–64, 76, 80, 82

Edwards, Harry, 13, 17, 74, 118
Evasion, 42, 52, 81, 85, 114, 120
Exclusion, 63, 102, 120
Exploit, 7, 10–14, 17, 19, 24, 31, 46, 60–61, 68, 78, 115, 121

Goffman, Erving, 3–4, 17, 104, 107, 117

Health insurance, 26–28

Identity, 16, 68, 79–80, 89–91, 94, 99, 118
Ideology, 5, 14–15, 19, 23, 62–63, 65–66, 68–69, 73–74, 76, 80–82, 85–86, 89, 110, 115, 120–121

Institutionalized, 17, 37, 61, 111, 117
Intersectionality, 79–80, 82

Labor, 5, 7, 9–12, 14–15, 33, 46, 49, 51, 57, 89

Marx, Karl, 10–13, 100n, 118
Masculinity, 5, 18–19, 62–63, 65–69, 71, 80, 110, 120
Methods, 15–16, 18

National Collegiate Athletic Association (NCAA), 2, 6, 17, 21, 115–117
Neoliberal, 4, 7–10, 14, 18–20, 24, 27, 37, 43, 74, 89, 103, 109–111, 114, 120
Neoliberal University (NLU), 1, 5, 15–18, 20, 29, 33, 73, 82–83, 100, 102, 103, 106
Norms, 3, 57, 60, 62, 65–67, 80, 87–89, 93, 95, 105, 113, 115, 119

Objectify, 26, 35, 40, 43–44, 60–61, 120
Organization, 2, 5, 8–9, 11, 14–15, 17, 22, 25–26, 29–30, 33, 35–40, 42, 51, 52, 54–58; racialized organization, 75, 82–83, 85, 120; gendered organization, 64, 68, 114
Oversee, 23–24, 76–77

Pain, 2, 41–42, 65–67, 69, 73, 77–78, 81, 92–95, 100–101, 104–107, 109, 111, 114–115, 120
Patriarchy, 14, 65–66, 85

Power, 2, 4–5, 10–12, 14, 16, 18–19, 24, 29, 33, 35–36, 39–40, 42, 44–45, 52, 53f, 54, 60, 71, 73–74, 78, 80–82, 89, 102, 110, 118–119
Privatize, 4, 8–9, 27–28. *See also* neoliberal
Profit, 2–4, 8, 14–15, 18–20, 26, 29–31, 35, 42, 46, 51–52, 54, 61, 71, 103, 109, 116
Profit-generating sport, 2, 3, 10, 12–14, 29–30, 34–35, 51, 65, 67–69, 71, 78, 80, 85, 102, 108, 114–115, 120–121; non-profit-generating sport, 31, 34–35, 48, 51, 68–69, 78, 80, 84, 114

Racialized, 10–13, 15, 18, 23, 61, 72–73, 76–78, 82–83, 85–86, 114, 120
Rationalization, 4, 14–15, 39, 57, 95. *See also* Max Weber
Reform, 115–118
Risk, 24, 67, 91, 94, 96; culture of risk, 93, 95, 114–115

Settler colonialism, 5–6, 10–11, 19, 74
Sports-industrial complex, 5–7, 19, 21, 28, 39, 120
Stereotype, 65, 69, 72–73, 79, 82, 85, 120

Title IX, 63–64, 79
Total institution, 3–4, 114. *See also* Erving Goffman
Trust, 43–46, 49

Weber, Max, 4, 15, 36, 39–40, 43, 95
Whiteness, 5, 18–19, 23, 73–75, 78, 80, 110

**Kaitlin Pericak** is Assistant Professor of Adult and Higher Education at the University of Oklahoma.

www.ingramcontent.com/pod-product-compliance
Lightning Source LLC
Chambersburg PA
CBHW020357170426
43200CB00005B/205